CUNARD

THE MOST FAMOUS OCEAN LINERS IN THE WORLD™

Library by Ocean Books

www.oceanbooks.com

BRIGHT LIGHTS, BIG CHANGES

Transatlantic Theatre
At The Turn Of Our Century

BRIGHT LIGHTS, BIG CHANGES

Transatlantic Theatre
At The Turn Of Our Century

By

Steven Rivellino

Library of Congress Number: 2004090103
ISBN :   Hardcover   1-4134-4480-6
              Softcover   1-4134-4479-2

Grateful acknowledgement is made to the Office of the Attorney General for the State of New York for the reprinting of their Executive Summary *Why Can't I Get Tickets?* — A Report on Ticket Distribution Practices Dated May 27, 1999. Copyright 1999 © All Rights Reserved.

1. Theatre—Broadway—Non Fiction. 2. Theatre—Off-Broadway—Non Fiction.
3. Theatre Criticism—Non Fiction. 4. Theatre—London—Non Fiction.
5. Theatre—The West End—Non Fiction. 6. Theatrical Producing—
Production—Non Fiction
7, Musical Theatre—Non Fiction.

First Edition
2004

www.brightlightsbigchanges.com

To order additional copies of this book, contact:
Xlibris Corporation
1-888-795-4274
www.Xlibris.com
Orders@Xlibris.com
23664

ALSO BY STEVEN RIVELLINO

Mysterious Places, Mysterious Dreams
A Novel Memoir

For Mom and Dad . . .

Contents

Introduction 11
   There's No Business Like Show Business

BROADWAY—
THAT'S WHERE I'D RATHER BE.

Part One— Traditions 15

A CANDID LOOK AT
LONDON'S WEST END

Part Two— All the World's a Stage 95

Part Three— At The End Of The Day 119

Appendix A 131
   Why Can't I Get Tickets?

Bibliography for *Bright Lights, Big Changes* 203

Special Thanks and Acknowledgments 205

About The Author 207

Notes on *Bright Lights, Big Changes* 208

Introduction—There's No Business Like Show Business

This is a book of one man's opinions.

There are many ways to produce a show. Indeed, producers work in different and various ways. And simply because one producer might prefer a specific style or tone or work process—and another not—does not necessarily make one producer right and the other wrong. There are no correct ways to produce a show.

Nonetheless, a well-produced show—a solid production creatively, physically, and fiscally responsible—can indeed help to make that show a success. While great producing will certainly not guarantee its success.

Indeed, over the years I've listened and I've observed and I've learned from the best. And by so doing—and from being fortunate enough to have been working continuously as an Executive Producer in all phases of the entertainment industry—I have witnessed true change in both direction and content for theatrical production over the years, on both sides of the Atlantic.

So herewith are my very own thoughts and observations taken from nearly twenty-five years in the industry. Herewith is my analysis.

Any errors or misstatements are therefore purely my own.

Indeed, theatre is a wonderful concept. It's about passion after all. And it has existed from time immemorial; since early man first told stories of heart-pounding hunts while perhaps drawing upon a cave wall his very own depiction of the one that got away.

Change is constant, and is pushed forth by many things. The economy, social mores, politics . . . just to name a few.

And the unthinkable can create change as well. Indeed, September 11, 2001 changed our world forever. But theatre succeeded well before that day. It continues strong today; and it will no doubt thrive far into the future. It will just be different, that's all. It can no longer be what it once was.

So let this book exist purely as a birthplace for thought—perhaps simply to get the dialogue going. Please think of it as a beginning; not an end.

And any assistance I might be in sparking an intelligent conversation about its future direction—well, that is all I can ask.

Steven Rivellino
February 2004

Broadway—
that's where I'd rather be.

January 2004

"Primum non nocere"
"First, do no harm"
—Hippocrates
Epidemics: Book 1, Section XI

Part One—Traditions

Not so long ago . . . the successful American Play wright Christopher Durang (*Sister Mary Ignatious Explains It All For You*, *The Marriage of Bette and Boo*) was quoted as saying

don't tell me Broadway's dying . . . it's already dead.

Just around that same time . . . the late great Broadway and television producer Alexander Cohen told a group of Theatre Arts Management Students:

Broadway is dedicated to commercial theatre. If you're
going to ask why Sam Shephard isn't produced on
Broadway today—well stop the nonsense
right now . . .
Broadway is a commercial institution. It has nothing
whatsoever to do with pretentious artistic notions. It's
there for one purpose, and one purpose
alone—to make money.

Now some might consider Messrs Cohen and Durang's words

15

a bit of an exaggeration; no doubt a bit cynical. But more and more people are indeed beginning to believe that Broadway is no longer about art and creativity and inventiveness—that it's actually about commercialism and commercialism alone. Indeed, if one were to look at what has been playing both on Broadway and in London's West End these last years, one would easily come to a similar conclusion.

But how did we get here, after all? How did London and New York—the true centers of theatrical creativity throughout history—certainly throughout the last century—move from often times earth-shaking emotional drama, to mediocre presentations and pure commercializations at best?

How have politics and contemporary world events affected this creativity? And how, if at all, will the theatre—as an entity—evolve and advance?

It is important, I think, to first explore a little bit of history. So let's start at the very beginning . . . indeed, it's a very good place to start. Let's begin where all shows begin—and that's with the producer.

Indeed, producers are an odd sort. Just ask Mel Brooks—or Richard Frankel or Barry Brown or even the ever-successful Cameron Mackintosh. Indeed, Max Bialystock might be a far far cry from reality; yet there is always some truth in good and everlasting comedy, and I'll just leave it at that.

Noted Broadway and film Producer Arthur Whitelaw (*Butterflies Are Free; The Taffettas; You're a Good Man Charlie Brown*) recently told an audience onboard Cunard Line's *Queen Elizabeth 2* that it was he, in fact, who burst into Alex Cohen's office one day in the early 1960s in utter panic—Alex being his mentor at the time—to advise that great producer that they had apparently *over*subscribed their investment on a recent project . . . they had indeed raised too much money; more money than they needed, or indeed should have raised.

"What shall we do?" the very young and eager Arthur Whitelaw asked his employer.

"Just leave it alone" Mr. Cohen is reportedly to have told the young man. "No one will know."

Oh—and I perhaps have forgotten to mention that seated in Mr. Cohen's office at the time was his great good friend Mel Brooks. And the rest, my dear reader, is film and theatrical history.

Nonetheless, shows indeed start and finish with the producer. He or she is the first to say "yes . . . let's do it." And the last to say " . . . close it tonight."

The Traditional Role of the Producer

Historically—simply put—a producer was just that. Someone who produced . . . someone who did it all.

I prefer to call him a *creative* producer. This was someone who first found a project—or a "property" as it is called in the industry; a property he or she truly believed in. There was an emotional attachment to the piece; one which drove the producer not only to believe that a particular play or musical should be produced on the great stages of the world, but made it a mission . . . a personal mission . . . to indeed make certain that his or her creative dream did in fact make it to Opening Night.

The producer's role was clear back then. He or she was responsible for it all. First, they optioned the property. Then, they worked with the writers to insure the script was refined as much as possible, certainly ready for the rehearsal room process.

Producers assembled the creative staff—the director, the scenic and lighting and costume designers; and on musicals—the choreographer, musical director, music and dance arrangers, too.

And they assembled the technical team—the Production Supervisor, carpenters, electricians, and their associated teams as well. In essence, producers were responsible for assembling and building the entire creative and technical package.

Producers were also responsible for general managing their shows as well. They handled the day-to-day administrative activity . . . contracts, payrolls, royalty distributions, box office settlements, house management, and on and on . . .

And on top of it all, producers produced the money.

Not so long ago, investment capital for Broadway productions was raised from individuals called "angels." And many of them there were.

I remember as a child opening *The New York Times* Arts and Leisure section and seeing enticing advertisements—"Investment Wanted for New Broadway Musical." The ad would reveal the upcoming show's branding logo, and offer potential investors the opportunity to write away for a Prospectus which would reveal all the necessary details for those patrons fantasizing about the great fame and glamour of being a part of a new Broadway show. Indeed, investment could only be made by Prospectus.

Often times, producers would produce what were called "Backer's Auditions." He or she would rent a large rehearsal space; assemble a team of potential actors to perform a scene or two from the play or musical in question, offering drinks of course to the invited guests, and the opportunity to meet and mix with the creative and overall management teams. Sometimes, these events were quite lavish evenings indeed, and were created solely as a solid attempt by the producer to entice would be investors to part with their money.

Monetary contributions in Broadway shows were—and still are today—partitioned as "units." But in those days, investment could be made for as little as $250 or $500. One could purchase as many units as one could afford; it was possible too to purchase a percentage of a unit as well, or split a unit amongst friends or colleagues.

Investors invested in theatre for many reasons. I doubt anyone truly believed that it was the best—or safest—investment one could make. Rather, they invested in theatre simply because they could. They loved the theatre. Indeed, they perhaps believed in the drama or musical project in consideration . . . trusted its writing; respected its creative and managerial teams; and simply went along for the ride. It was fun, after all, to be a part of that team. It was exciting too to feel that close to creativity, albeit at an investors arm-length. And it was pride too which excited them about attending Opening Night Galas; to sit at Sardis with the stars of *their* show awaiting the very first edition of the following day's *The New York Times* or other such paper of theatrical critical distinction on Opening Night. Would we be a hit? Or was it disaster?

But that's all gone now.

Why? Basic Economics. Let's take a brief look at the history . . .

Hey Big Spender

In 1967, the production costs of a typical Broadway musical was $500,000.

In 1975, that cost doubled to $1,000,000.

By 1982—the production costs for Cameron Mackintosh's highly anticipated musical *Miss Saigon* were estimated at $10,000,000. That's right . . . in eight years, the cost of a Broadway show increased ten-fold. And that was for a show that was already "produced" and highly successful in the West End; all production challenges were already solved and finalized; it was essentially a remount of an already existing show. In fact, the New York production of *Miss Saigon* was actually scaled back a bit from the original production in order to accommodate a somewhat smaller stage at New York's Broadway Theatre.

And 1998 brought us Disney's *The Lion King*—with production costs estimated at between $15,000,000 and $20,000,000.

So here we are; and what, indeed, have we all created?

Clearly, when a typical Broadway drama can cost in excess of $5,000,000; and a musical in the tens of millions range—the production process simply had to change. It's not only difficult but perhaps downright impossible for an individual producer of any stature to raise or invest himself $10M on such speculation. Imagine the number of "angels" it would take to reach such an investment goal, to capitalize such a venture.

And in addition to it all, producers have to formally file with New York State's Attorney Generals office—or worse, with the United States Securities and Exchange Commission (SEC)—for approval to raise such funds; clearly, a labor-and-cost-intensive—and time-consuming—task in itself. If any of you have seen an SEC Prospectus for a Broadway production from the 1980s-1990s, no doubt you would have been intimidated right from the opening paragraph on page one. Before any investment details were even listed about the particular show in question, the SEC offered at least ten reasons why a potential investor should not invest in a Broadway show; that he or she should indeed expect total loss of investment. Certainly, not a user-friendly document, to say the least.

Obviously, these practices began to scare the traditional (individual) Broadway investors away, and quickly eliminated the opportunity for any new individual investors as well.

It created then, a need for a new type of Producer.

There's Safety In Numbers

Today, Broadway shows are essentially produced by committee—put together by what one might call Production Conglomerates; "big money"-type investors—either individual or corporate. And as such, investment is usually achieved in quite large sums—$1M to $3M per "investor."

In a 2002 interview with Playbill.com's Robert Simonson, noted director/producer Hal Price said "I went to see a show last winter. Good play. And there were twenty-three producers' names over the title. First I smiled and thought Gee, I hope they win the Tony because I want to see that with my own eyes. And then I thought, what is that? What does that say about producing?"

"You can't have producing by committee" Mr. Prince continued. "And we need creative producers. That is a breed that still exists, of course, but in smaller numbers than when there were single people and partners presenting plays. I would love to see a modicum of that in the business [today]."

The result of this change in production investing has essentially revolutionized the industry. Why? With money, comes power. And anyone (individual or group) willing to invest such large sums of money is no doubt going to want to have a say in how that money is spent; in how his investment will be used.

And so the power has shifted—shifted, indeed. The decision-makers of today are not necessarily like those who passionately believed in their creative project as the great producers of the past. The power now lies in the hands of those with the largest pocketbooks. And unfortunately—most often—those with the largest pocketbooks are not necessarily those who harbor the most creative instincts. Those with the needed funds do not necessarily understand how important it is to nurture a script throughout the creative process; to guide its development solidly to Opening Night.

And so most theatre professionals today—renowned fixtures within the industry, for sure—believe that this new production process to be quite dangerous for the future of the industry.

Whose Show Is It Anyway?

It's clear we're finding more and more corporate conglomerates producing on Broadway today. These corporations or "production entities" as they are sometimes called are made up of those whose sole responsibility is most likely to the bottom line. Their role could have several agendas—naturally, to return solid investment to their owners or stockholders, but they might also hold a deeper agenda as well.

Massive corporate entities like Clear Channel Entertainment, Cablevision, and Disney Theatricals too, have all stuck their wandering toes into the investment pool called Broadway. Some have succeeded, others not. Some work to feed their other corporate entities with product . . . as is the case with Clear Channel who not only produces "product", but enjoys the luxury of owning many of the national theatres in which their productions might play. One theatrical hand, no doubt, washing the other.

Disney, of course, has an even greater purpose. Yes, I'm certain, their Theatrical Division must indeed return a profit to the mother-company and their eager investors. But they are also able to synergize their properties from one creative format to another. For example—the massive success of the marvelous film *Beauty and the Beast* allowed Disney Theatricals to take an already successful creative property and beautifully transform it to the Broadway stage, and subsequently to international stages as well. And such was a similar practice they followed, of course, with *The Lion King*. What's further on their agenda? *Aladdin, The Little Mermaid,* and perhaps *Pinocchio* too. All solid properties; all housing little risk as well due to their already well-known and widely praised storylines.

Other film companies too have found a desire to be a part of the great white way. Fox Theatricals—at the talented hand of former Fox executive and first-time theatrical producer Lindsay Law—was able to brilliantly transform their successful film *The Full Monty* into a marvelously written, directed, staged, and produced theatrical success—clearly one of the best American musicals in years. And with the great success of the film version of the Kander and Ebb musical *Chicago*, no doubt Miramax will be swimming more often with the Broadway sharks as well.

More and more, we are finding that film companies will "option" or license the Broadway rights to a property, inexpensively securing them then for future film production. They might not necessarily care about, or be mainly concerned with, the quality or success of the Broadway production itself, but in trying out the creative, if you will—to see if audiences accept it. In effect, it is far less expensive to produce a Broadway show these days, than a major Hollywood film. And that, we all know, is where they believe their *true* profits can be made.

In addition, we are seeing more and more that Broadway production today is daringly taken on by a very small segment of the population—perhaps a segment one would least expect. And some extremely wealthy individuals with little else to do with their funds but invest in Broadway musicals are beginning to do just that. Those who perhaps have always felt a kinship with the arts; who perhaps simply want to be a part of something as exciting and as creative as a Broadway production. Those who might know little about the business of producing shows, or in the creative art itself.

We're finding that many of these nouveau-riche impresarios of the 00s might indeed have the money, but clearly lack the experience. They might be able to bankroll a project from inception to closing curtain, but have little understanding of how to develop and grow the creative—in essence, in some cases, dooming a project before it even has a chance to sprout.

Why Have Production Costs Escalated As They Have?

" . . . She wants life to be romantic and magical but the sordid, gritty side rears its head at her every step of the way. . . . Death is expensive, Miss Stella."

Indeed, Tennessee Williams knew of which he spoke in his 1947 masterpiece *A Streetcar Named Desire (A Streetcar Named Desire* played on Broadway at the Ethel Barrymore Theatre from Dec 3, 1947 through Dec 17, 1949).

And so it is as one would expect. The costs of a Broadway show these days have escalated tremendously over the years. In particular, it's the costs of the physical production of any show which has unkindly tipped the balance sheet. Lighting equipment, scenery, costumes, props, and lavish special effects too have all contributed to making the cost of a contemporary Broadway show out of reach for most individual independent producers.

Indeed, things cost what they cost. There's just no way of getting around it. And it's not only the costs of the materials themselves, it's the construction and fabrication as well. All physical elements for such shows must, of course, be built in union shops. And as we all know, union costs are continually on the rise.

Naturally, unions had their place in American history. Indeed, even today, unions are necessary and can be quite helpful on both sides of the equation—not only to protect working conditions and employee benefits, but for management as well. I know from my own experience, I prefer to work with union labor under union agreements since it offers me the opportunity to work with highly skilled personnel with pre-agreed-upon rules and rates. In a way, it makes things pretty straight-forward—as straight-forward perhaps as anything can ever get in this business.

But unions too can be unrealistic, and have sometimes been known to provoke quite nasty encounters between labor and management. Unfortunately, those incidents are the ones which stay in most people's minds, and conjure up quite a negative image of what union relations can mean.

A Benevolent Brotherhood Of Man

2003 saw two highly-publicized union-induced work actions in New York—the results of which, I'm afraid, will have lasting impressions on the industry as a whole.

Early that year, Broadway experienced a near weeklong work-stoppage (March 7th through March 11th) initiated by musicians union Local 802. Ironically, salaries were not the main issue, but rather work security; a guarantee of employment—something unheard of anywhere in the open marketplace.

There are two types of Broadway theatres: musical houses and dramatic houses. And Musicians Local 802 has imposed a labor "minimum call" on all musical houses in New York City based on the size of the audience—the larger the house, the more musicians must be engaged.

A producer booking one of the so-designated "musical houses" is required then to engage that minimum number of musicians so imposed by Local 802, whether or not that number of musicians is actually needed.

Similarly—a producer who might decide to book a "musical house" for a dramatic production (perhaps because a suitable "dramatic house" might not be available) would also be required to engage that theatre's musician's minimum, whether they worked the show or not.

Naturally, as musical styles and tastes have changed, so should union terms. It is far more typical these days to have a complement of ten or twelve musicians in the pit of a typical

Broadway musical; the need, therefore, for larger orchestras has lessened due to the type of music being written.

Nonetheless, Local 802 is a powerful force in the entertainment and theatrical industries, so there voice became quite loud in the media. And as the musicians threatened to strike and close down Broadway until they got their way, producers too threatened to record their show's orchestrations and continue to perform without live musicians at all.

So 802 decided to strike. But with the potential use of the newly recorded musical tracks in the producer's back pocket, the expected impact of the strike was minimal. That is, of course, until the other theatrical unions (Actor's Equity Association and IATSE—the International Alliance of Theatre Stage Employees Local 1) voted to support the picket line and their fellow union brothers and sisters.

By this point in the negotiations the talks became heated, and the New York media loved every moment. Eventually, a compromise was reached. Producers agreed not to use recorded musical tracks; 802 maintained their "minimums" although fewer musicians than originally partitioned did indeed get their guarantees. Producers were able to achieve just *some* operational savings in the settlement.

The same season saw a highly publicized walkout by the world famous Radio City Rockettes®, also for reasons of employment guarantees. It seems difficult to image a troupe of dancers—no matter how proficient or internationally celebrated—could reasonably demand a guarantee of lifetime employment with utter disregard to the very real practicalities of advancing age or weight or other physical attrition. However, in this instance, management won—successfully disbanding the Rockette's employment seniority roster which had been in place for decades.

Similar labor/management disagreements continue throughout the industry. And the impracticality of some still archaic work rules—not only within the Musicians Local 802 or the Rockettes' American Guild of Variety Artists (AGVA), but with other union affiliations as well—help to contribute to shows closing far earlier than they should, or indeed—to some shows never getting produced at all.

Magic To Do

Before a show ever sees the lights of Broadway, one of the first things prepared is, of course, the budget. A producer must first assess the financial practicality of his proposed production before responsibly moving ahead. And there are actually two very different budgets necessary for the mounting of any Broadway show.

The Production Budget is the account of any and all start-up costs, creative costs, physical costs, rehearsal costs, and all operational costs leading up to Opening Night.

The Weekly Operating Budget accounts for the weekly expenditures needed to keep the show up and running for a standard eight-performance week.

These budgets are quite lengthy and detailed, with constant consideration made to the size of the theatre in which the show will be presented, and the number of potential seats available for sale resulting, of course, in potential revenue.

In reviewing a budget for any Broadway show, several line-items will inevitably jump out. As one might expect, the largest numbers will no doubt be in the scenic and costume design and production categories; labor will be up there as well.

But perhaps somewhat surprisingly, one of the largest numbers one will see in any Broadway Production Budget today will be for Advertising and Marketing. For it is here where the success of a show can truly be made or broken.

It all began in November 1972. A new musical was slated to open on Broadway called *Pippin*—a rather intriguing piece with book by Roger O. Hirson and music and lyrics by a new and very young composer named Stephen Schwartz. *Pippin* was set to open at Broadway's Imperial Theatre—produced by Stuart Ostrow; directed and choreographed by the late great Bob Fosse.

Most students of theatre will know that *Pippin* was not particularly well-received. In fact, critical reviews for the show were fair to mixed at best—so mixed, that after a month or two of struggling at the box office—and soon approaching the notoriously poor-selling Christmas/New Year Holiday week—Ostrow's uniquely-conceived new musical was literally on the verge of closing.

It was, in fact, the imaginative Bob Fosse who first saw the merit and great opportunity in the rather simplistic storyline by Messrs Hirson and Schwartz. So it was not surprising that it was Bob Fosse who also first had the idea that would change theatrical history.

After convincing Stuart Ostrow to invest even more cash into his flailing production, Fosse took one of his lead characters—The Leading Player (a very young Ben Vereen, at the time)—and two of his principle dancers into a cold New York city sound stage and filmed one of the most brilliant and intriguing choreographic segments in the show . . . the very imaginative "Manson Trio" as it is now known to many throughout the industry. And by so doing, Bob Fosse created the very first television commercial ever produced for a Broadway Show. The rest, as they say, is theatrical history.

Pippin ran for four and a half years on the Great White Way; and that sixty-second film changed forever the way Broadway shows would be marketed.

Give 'Em The Old Razzle Dazzle

Today, it is inconceivable for any producer worth his weight to attempt to mount a Broadway production without having the foresight—and the budget—to market his show appropriately. For a musical, television advertising is a given; at the least, full-page print ads in not only *The Sunday New York Times* but in other popular periodicals as well are the minimum necessary.

There's also Metro bus and bus-stop signage, subway signage, radio spots, "the making of" television specials—and on and on it goes. And indeed, the budgets keep rising. But the impact is key. The idea is to keep the show in the public's mind as much as possible. The name recognition is most important. The more knowledge the public might have of a new show, the more expansive their comfort level. Box office records indicate that we're living in a society that buys tickets to see only the shows with which they are familiar. And if it takes millions of dollars to create and maintain that awareness, well so be it.

And The Money Keeps Rolling In

It's becoming clear as well that clever marketing campaigns (advertising *and* public relations working synergistically) can not only sell your show well, but might even be able to take a show which perhaps might have been poorly received by the critics, and turn it into a name-brand success.

Take, for example, the musical *Footloose* which opened on Broadway in the autumn of 1998. The show was produced by Dodgers Theatricals, directed by Walter Bobbie and choreographed by A.C. Ciulla. *Footloose* received, perhaps, the worst reviews of any show this author has seen in his lifetime . . . *Carrie* and perhaps *Moose Murders* notwithstanding.

" . . . Footloose, the flavorless marshmallow of a musical that opened last night at the Richard Rodgers' Theatre . . ."

"There have certainly been worse musicals on Broadway than Footloose . . . yet it's hard to think of one so totally unaffecting."

" . . . this production has a blurry, removed feeling, like a Xerox of a Polaroid."

" . . . Footloose has a perverse tendency to muffle the endings of its songs, as though it weren't really expecting much applause."

—Ben Brantley for *The New York Times* October 23, 1998 –
Late Edition Final. Section E, Column 4, Page 1.

With those notices, most producers would have closed that show in an instant; certainly on Opening Night. But here were producers . . . albeit a "corporate" entity, but an entertainment-based entity nonetheless . . . who stood solidly behind their product. They challenged the critics; and believed their show had potential. Word of mouth was key, they believed. And all they needed to do was to get people into the theatre.

So Dodgers Theatricals went ahead and invested even *more* money into their seemingly doomed production—targeting a specific audience segment. Indeed, teenagers—teenage girls, to be specific— were the basis for their very ingenious marketing plan. After all, boy bands were all the rage back then . . . why not focus on that specific market segment and maximize its potential?

TV ads for Footloose soon focused-in on this specific segment of the audience; sexy boy band-type photos and related advertising placed in key teen magazines and other publications also supported the plan.

In addition, they staged a uniquely conceived finale "tag"—

featuring the very young and sexy male lead, together with four of his equally young and sexy male buddies, in a rousing, well-choreographed "closer" which literally got the teens screaming, and symbolically brought down the house.

Strategic brilliance? Clearly. Luck? No doubt. And it worked.

Footloose ran at the Richard Rodgers Theatre for two and one-half years—creating, then, a superb market for touring and other such companies worldwide.

A lesson to be learned, no doubt. Thank you Dodger Theatricals. Let's hear it for the boy . . .

Star Light / Star Bright . . .

> **Star** n. a very famous, successful, and popular performer, especially in the field of entertainment or sports
>
> n. somebody who is particularly good at some activity, or who is the most important or most skillful member of a group involved in a particular activity
>
> adj. Very or most important, skillful, or successful
>
> v. to have somebody as the leading performer or as one of the leading performers
>
> v. to be the leading performer or one of the leading performers in something such as a movie or play

> —*The American Heritage® Dictionary of the English Language*
> Fourth Edition. Copyright © 2000 by Houghton Mifflin Company.
> Published by the Houghton Mifflin Company. All rights reserved.

In the 1950s, a young Marilyn Monroe slithered seductively on the great silver screen as she sang "Diamonds are a girls best friend." We'll let's just say that today in our industry, stars might be considered a producer's best friend. And when producers are successful at engaging stars for their productions, many of them slither as well.

So just how important is a "star" in today's theatrical marketplace?

No doubt it is perhaps the spark of many a legend in the industry that stars are a pain in the proverbial ass. Indeed, such horror stories have been bandied about for decades. But I have to say that I've had marvelous experiences with "stars" throughout my career. The one or two whose light may not shine as bright, need not be mentioned here.

But stars do in fact often translate to solid box office receipts. And so on the theatrical stages of Broadway and London's West End, I'm afraid to say that stars are here to stay. They make a show more than just a show, but an event—a "must see" attraction.

But often times, along with the good, also comes the bad—and the bad usually relates to money. The fees such celebrities are paid for their performing services onstage cause producers great headache. It's true that compared to film, Broadway numbers might be considered a pittance. But when you take into consideration the differences in scale—what the potential revenue might be from a blockbuster film and what its counterpart might indeed be on the Great White Way— one quickly realizes the dilemma we've created.

But there is a Catch-22 here; at least in many contemporary producers' minds. What good is a play, after all—no matter how well written or how well produced, or how well directed—if it doesn't sell. If there's no name above the title? No "star" to cause a solid box office stampede? Why take the risk then with any production that it will be able to sell tickets on its own merit? Go the star route; it just might be the only way to go.

And so, we see producers today fighting a no win battle of sorts. How to convince a star to do one's show without having to pay the exorbitant sums associated with such contracts. We've come to the point, I'm afraid, were it seems as if the star is becoming far more important than the play itself. Sounds a bit like the old "tail wagging the dog" theory to me.

Now let there be no doubt that in the pure sense of the word a star is a star . . . but a Broadway star today might have little relationship to one's image of what the traditional Broadway star might have been.

Take for example the legendary Ethel Merman vs. today's Brandy.

Laurence Olivier vs. Tom Selleck.

Angela Landsbury vs. Rosie O'Donnell.

Ezio Pinza vs. Sean Combs (also known as Puff Daddy and/or P. Diddy).

Indeed, the Broadway star of today might be someone far less than one would expect. So lets, for the purpose of this discussion not call them stars at all, but celebrities. Indeed, they are more TV star than stage diva; more rock star than classically-trained thespian. But for the sake of this discussion, let's put basic talent skills aside, and delve into an issue perhaps far more important to producers today. And that's the issue of money.

Celebrities who star in Broadway shows today can easily earn in excess of $75,000 to $100,000 per week. And when you're looking at an average weekly "break even" cost of $500,000 for a musical—that's 20% of the production's overall financial nut.

Rumor had it that when Bernadette Peters' contract for her leading role in the 2000 revival of *Annie Get Your Gun* was coming to a close, the notorious husband and wife producing team of Barry and Fran Weissler looked high and low for a star replacement of considerable name and box office value. After a long and tedious search, they decided to offer the leading role to Dolly Parton—

certainly a "star" in anyone's book; certainly one who would drive great box office in theatrical circles anywhere. Actually, it was a brilliant decision. Parton's would be a novelty performance at best, nonetheless one well suited for that popular revival of Irving Berlin's classic; one which might sell-out for months.

So the Weisslers—not known within the industry to be the most "generous" of producers—negotiated with Ms. Parton's management for an apparent $125,000 per week; quite a large sum for most Broadway pockets.

Apparently however, after Ms. Parton finally agreed to the offer, she then set forth one of her key terms—she would only perform three shows per week; not the usual eight performances per week—the industry standard. Clearly, not acceptable. Clearly, the end of the deal.

And so the frantic search for a replacement celebrity continued until the very popular country performer Reba Macintyre was cast and soon had critics raving. Clearly, Ms. Macintyre was the right choice after all. The Weisslers are no fools.

It was the Weisslers, after all, who might be responsible for letting this celebrity craze get out of the bag, if you will. One could look back to their 1994 revival of the Jim Jacobs/Warren Casey musical *Grease* as the time and date it might all have begun.

That show became a veritable revolving door of celebrities, that's for sure—Rosie O'Donnell, Brooks Shield, Sheena Easton— just to name a few. All *pop* celebrities for sure. All known perhaps *solely* for their celebrity. Few with any respectable legitimate acting credits; few who would be able to command the stage on his or her own merit.

But perhaps a fun and flippant musical like *Grease* just might be able to get away with such novelty casting far more than something a bit more serious, more dramatic. Casting for the glitz of it all, one might say. And in the case of *Grease* such novelty casting proved a success; indeed, the Weissler's revival of *Grease* ran on Broadway from 1994 to 1998–1505 performances. And so the celebrity race began . . .

The 2002-2003 Broadway season brought one of the most anticipated openings in recent Broadway history—the return of the Tony Award-winning *Phantom of the Opera* himself.

Michael Crawford had not performed on Broadway since his 1988 characterization as that masked man from deep below the Paris Opera House. So any return to the New York stage for Mr. Crawford would naturally draw some eager attention from fans and critics alike.

It was interesting to note, however, that the musical he chose for his long-awaited return to Broadway was the long-running German musical sensation *Dance Of The Vampires*. Why ever would the Tony-winning star choose such a piece? Too much wolf-bane, perhaps? You're guess is as good as mine. Perhaps Mr. Crawford and the entire creative team thought that his return to the Great White Way as yet another creature who lives alone in the dark—who also stalks a pretty young maiden—would be of great interest to his fans. And how wrong they were.

> "Michael Crawford, who sported a dashing half-mask for his Tony-winning performance in The Phantom of the Opera in 1988, would have done well to have donned a fuller version for his return to Broadway. Rigged up as a taxidermic variation on his Phantom persona, Mr. Crawford opened last night in a show called Dance of the Vampires at the Marquis Theater. It is an enterprise to be associated with only under the veil of anonymity."

> "No one, even after a quart of straight gin, would be able to erase the memory of Mr. Crawford as a blood-sucking

aristocrat and Mandy Gonzalez as his toothsome prey, shrieking a revised version of Mr. [Jim] Steinman's pop hit *Total Eclipse of the Heart*. The scene is perfectly accessorized by a phalanx of pasty, hooded creatures, holding (I swear) what appear to be flashlights beneath their faces, like monsters in a homemade spook house."

Ben Brantley for *The New York Times*
December 10, 2002. © 2002—All Rights Reserved.

"Few musicals in recent years have created the expectations of *Dance of the Vampires*. No one, mind you, expected anything good. But based on advance reports, many nurtured the hope that Vampires might be truly awful, like the legendary *Carrie: The Musical.*

"It is my sad duty to report that, although the writing is amateurish and vulgar, the music mindless and the acting—for the most part—ludicrously broad, *Vampires* does not reach the *Carrie* threshold of awfulness. . . . this failure stems from its halfheartedness."

Howard Kissel for *The New York Daily News*
December 10, 2002. © 2002 – All Rights Reserved.

So the critics were not pleased. That's clear—across the board. And so with little advance ticket revenue in the bank, the multi-million dollar spectacle was doomed.

Ironic it is then that *Vampire*'s producers were so confident of their success that the structured a very unusual and quite lucrative financial deal for Mr. Crawford in order to entice him to star in their show. Several sources have reported that Mr. Crawford was offered an enormous weekly salary of nearly $180,000 to appear in the ill-fated musical, with perks—apparently including retirement annuities and more—pushing well into the millions. For Mr. Crawford—it was perhaps an unfortunate creative choice (which most likely cost him the starring role in the film version of *The Phantom Of The Opera*); for the producers of *Dance of the Vampires*—it was quite an unwise deal if indeed true.

Standing on the Corner

There are several aspects of theatrical production that perhaps most people would not even think about when calculating a show's weekly operating costs. Take real estate, for example.

Today, all Broadway theatres are owned by the Shubert Organization, the Nederlanders, The Jujamcyn Group—and now, most recently, by Disney Theatricals and Clear Channel Entertainment.

Anyone who lives anywhere in this world will know that real estate costs are continually increasing. And perhaps no one knows that better than New Yorkers. Such costs include not only New York City Real Estate Tax (which, by the way, mandated quite a large boost in 2003), but also the costs of heating, air conditioning, water, permits, electrical, etc.

The result of such increases in house costs—real estate costs— is indeed quite interesting to assess, for again, it's changed the way we do business.

Producers, you see, are not the only ones eager to make money. Theatre owners too are concerned with their investment. And naturally, as their costs rise, so too do the costs to the producers who may attempt to rent that landlord's facility for his or her new production.

Theatre owners have a unique point of view—a conundrum which most certainly effects the lives of Broadway producers and the audience as well. Naturally, they want to see their "house" booked for as long a period as possible. So they will be interested, of course, in renting their house to the show which they feel has indeed the most chances of succeeding that season. It's not uncommon, then, for a theatre owner to deny a producer's request to rent his facility if, for some arbitrary reason, the theatre owner deems that particular show not worthy of succeeding. In a way, then, it could be said that theatre owners have some say in what you—the theatre-going-public—get to see. If the production is not necessarily "up their alley"—well then . . . good luck Mr. Producer. You and your show will be homeless, for sure.

Recently, you may have noticed that some theatre owners are finding more and more creative ways to increase revenue. And so there has been a popular trend to take on corporate sponsors.

Several years ago, the Canadian-based production juggernaut Livent (which was taken over by Clear Channel Entertainment a few years back) named their new home on 42nd Street the Ford Center for the Performing Arts; the Ford Corporation putting up much, if not most, of the construction costs.

The Roundabout Theatre Company quickly followed suit when they bought and refurbished the former Selwyn Theatre, also on New York's 42nd Street. In a glorious ceremony, they christened their new theatre the American Airlines/Selwyn Theatre. Both the Roundabout Theatre Company and American Airlines together, doing what they do best.

And most recently, the Shubert Organization crowned the elegant marquee atop Broadway's classic Winter Garden Theatre with proud new signage announcing The Cadillac Winter Garden. Mamma mia!

At the 2001 groundbreaking ceremony for the newly redesigned/refurbished Biltmore Theatre, Manhattan Theatre Club Board Chairman Peter J. Solomon said that MTC was actively seeking individuals and/or corporations for donations in exchange for what's come to be known as "naming opportunities."

"You give me $10 million" Mr. Solomon said, "you [can] have the name [on the marquee], the lobby, and the first five rows [of seats]."

Money, Money, Money

The trick is to follow the money. And when you do, you'll soon see that the money keeps rolling in. Because as we all know—ticket prices have skyrocketed.

Let's take a quick look . . .

In 1967, the cost of a Saturday evening orchestra seat for a new musical on Broadway was $15.00.

In 1975, that same ticket—for the original production of Bob Fosse's *Chicago*—rose to $17.50.

In 1980, a Saturday evening orchestra seat for a new Broadway musical was set at $27.50.

By 1980, the cost of that same seat jumped to $47.50.

In 1991—for Cameron Mackintosh's newest musical *Miss Saigon*—the Saturday evening orchestra ticket price was $60.00.

And in 1998, for the Pulitzer Prize-winning musical *Rent*, a Saturday evening orchestra seat was selling for $80.00.

Soon, the proverbial glass chandelier would smash through the ceiling. It was a dreaded expectation, but one we all saw coming. And it happened in celebration of the new Mel Brooks Musical *The Producers*—when they began offering their orchestra tickets for $100.00. Richard Frankel and his team of producers even began selling special VIP tickets for $450.00. That's what happens when you win all the Tony Awards, and then some. You get greedy. But as we all know, greed sometimes spreads like maggots on a dead whale carcass. And when the producers of *The Producers* raised the price bar, others felt the need to jump over as well.

And so today, there it is. First-time producer Rosie O'Donnell began selling tickets to her new Broadway musical *Taboo* for $101.25. And others soon joined her. Tickets to most Broadway musicals at the time of this writing are $100+ across the board. No ifs, ands, or buts.

Disney's *The Lion King* — $110.00
Disney's *Aida* — $105.00
Never Gonna Dance — $101.25

Even some dramas have not been spared. *Cat On A Hot Tin Roof* (Revival 2003)—although advertising tickets for $86.25, is currently offering "premium" orchestra seats for $151.25

Just think about the situation higher and higher ticket pricing is creating. Think about the average theatergoer; how laying out those kinds of dollars might impact his life. In 2003, a night at the theatre could easily exceed $450—when one takes into consideration a New York City dinner for two, parking perhaps, a babysitter . . . Not a simple sum for most to spend for a night on the town.

And the result? That same theatergoer might not be able to see as many shows each season as he (or the producers, in fact) would like. And in addition, he will no doubt want to insure that his $100-$110 per theatre ticket investment is well spent.

An audience member might only be willing to take limited risk at those prices. And therefore, might only be interested in seeing the "hit" of the season. The more interesting—perhaps, more thought provoking—productions then could easily fall by the wayside.

So I'm afraid that what we're seeing more and more of these days is a Broadway which is far more "mass market" in content, with across the board appeal. Nothing daring. Nothing challenging. Just fine, that's all. Just fine.

In essence, I think producers have put themselves in a bit of a bind. Some feel that if the theatre audiences are *un*willing to take risks with their "ticket" investment, then they—the producers themselves—are more and more *un*willing to take risks with *their* investment—the production itself.

After all . . . only one in four musicals ever break-even, let alone show a profit.

And so we have the dilemma.

Indeed, the days of the great "hands-on" producers are gone. David Merrick; Robert Whitehead; Hal Prince (as producer); Bob Fosse (as a producer); and even perhaps the great impresario himself, Joseph Papp. Back in their heyday, those names on a marquee meant something. It told the ticket buyer that the play they were about to see would be intelligent. It would be passionate. And perhaps most of all, it would be about *something*. It would make the audience feel happy or sad . . . it might even make them angry. But it would do its damnedest to make them care about what was happening up there on that stage. Call it "theatre involvement" if you will.

Indeed, those producers took risks with the projects they believed in, and by so doing, we ended up with some pretty magnificent theatre.

In the 2002 *New York Times* obituary for producer Robert Whitehead, the great American playwright Arthur Miller said "Mr. Whitehead was one of a handful of producers . . . who longed for artistically ambitious and socially interesting plays, and could put their money where their mouth was."

Yes, back then, producers helped to create an atmosphere in which there existed an audience for shows other than the hits of the season. And that was a very healthy atmosphere indeed.

Today, it's rare to see a producer willing to take risks.

Most Broadway productions at the turn of this century will not even see the light of day without first passing through what's called a workshop.

Ah yes . . . the workshop. A rather interesting concept most likely created by producers and directors who are uncomfortable trusting the content of their writer's own word.

So off they go . . . producer, director, choreographer, writers, designers, and full cast too—off to a rehearsal space somewhere as far from civilization as can be. And there they could settle-in for weeks, months . . . and sometimes even longer than that; doors closed, voices raised. And over and over again they test, and they prod, and they re-write, and they try it again, and they test some more, and re-write once again. Let's keep doing it until we get it right.

But is it ever really *right*, or do you just stop?

There are many ways, at least, to *try* to get it right.

Garth Drabinsky—former Chief Executive and renowned impresario of the now defunct Toronto-based production company Livent Inc.—found a rather unique method of "getting it right." But before we discuss the details . . . a little background on Mr. Drabinsky.

The last decade of the twentieth century brought little originality to the theatrical world. Few new and exciting ideas ever reached the lights of Broadway. Most producers perhaps were just a bit too cautious to try anything new; many were intimidated by the overwhelming success of Cameron Mackintosh's mega hits of the time.

But there was one ray of sunshine on that darkened page in theatrical history. And many industry insiders—somewhat secretly, at least— did consider Livent Inc. to be the one great hope for a renewed theatrical industry here in North America; and Mr. Drabinsky was its fair-haired boy.

Having first put *Cineplex Odeon* on the film industry's map (1984) creating North America's second-largest movie-theatre chain, Garth Drabinsky took his extraordinary experience and highly skilled management team full-speed into the live theatrical world (1989). The success of his celebrated production of the Tony Award-winning *Kiss of the Spider Woman* clearly set Livent's sails aflutter, and off they went on a remarkable international producing spree.

Although Livent was a publicly-held/publicly-traded company (1993) with many energized stockholders eager to turn a quick profit, Mr. Drabinsky was certainly not your typical corporate CEO. In fact, Drabinsky was one of those creative producers I discussed at the beginning of this book—perhaps the last of that great breed. With all the bravado of the old-time impresarios, Garth Drabinsky brought intense passion with him from the cinema world. He seemed unafraid of theatrical risk and was openly willing to produce the projects he truly believed in. And he was dedicated to his passions as well—following-through to spectacular completion.

In assembling the creative team for his blockbuster production of *Ragtime* (Stephen Flaherty & Lynn Ahrens, Terrance McNally, Frank Galati, Graciela Daniele, Eugene Lee, Santo Loquasto, Jules Fisher & Peggy Eisenhower), Drabinsky clearly chose the best. And in the true spirit of the traditional (theatrical) production practices of the past, Mr. Drabinsky solidly believed in his team and their unique abilities to tell that story well.

"Garth implicitly trusted every creative member of that team" Stephen Flaherty recently told me. "He maintained unwavering passion for our show right from the beginning; he supported us all in every way possible so that we were free to tell the story we all wanted to tell."

Yet that creative team was not so easy to assemble. E.L. Doctorow— author of the original novel—was apparently not too pleased with the film version of *Ragtime* which had been produced several years before. So when it came time to create the theatrical version, Mr. Doctorow wanted to be directly involved in the "casting" of his (and Mr. Drabinsky's) theatrical storytellers.

That creative team, in fact, literally had to audition for their roles—something which rarely, if ever, happens in the theatre today. There were ten musical teams, in fact, who were being considered to write the music and lyrics for *Ragtime*. Stephen Flaherty and Lynn Ahrens wrote four songs "on speculation"— so eager and passionate they were to be a part of that amazing and challenging new project. And rightly so . . . they were chosen hands-down as *the team* to musicalize Messrs Doctorow and Drabinsky's theatrical vision.

But corporate pressures are ever-present . . . and Garth Drabinsky headed a corporation after all. With all his passion, and with all his good will, he still had stockholders pounding at his door; watching his every move. Livent's investment in *Ragtime* was huge. And with the opening night glamour gone, and the prestige of having invested in perhaps the hottest new show in town pushed aside, financial "return on investment" was most often on their minds.

Garth was thrilled with the show his team had created, and he felt the advertising campaign needed to be just as spectacular as the show itself; something unusual, truly unique. But advertising campaigns cost money, and *Ragtime* was already far overdrawn.

So Garth returned to his corporation [and his stockholders] to request additional investment. And in support of his argument, he utilized the results of a marketing technique so commonplace in the cinema world—polling the audience.

During preview performances of *Ragtime* at Toronto's Ford Center for the Performing Arts, Garth distributed lengthy questionnaires to his eager audience groups. If he could determine what they *really* thought of his new show . . . only then, he felt, would he be able to determine the best ways to advertise and market his newest production.

So audiences in essence became producers—at least in the marketing sense. Indeed, they got their chance to tell Mr. Drabinsky just what they did in fact think of his new musical. Everything was rated—the scenery, the costumes, the music and the lyrics . . . they were even asked to offer comments on the performers themselves.

And Garth got a windfall. And he used that information not only to determine how best to market his show (what audiences responded to most enthusiastically, etc.), but also to calm his very nervous corporate investors by showing them that the feedback they were getting from their preview audiences was indeed overwhelmingly positive, supporting of course Mr. Drabinsky's request for additional advertising funds over and above the original production budget allotment.

Now let there be no doubt that this can be a very dangerous practice indeed; creatively, at least. One thing we all learned in elementary school was that when you ask ten people their opinions, you might in fact receive ten *different* opinions. What one person might like, another might despise. But that doesn't necessarily mean that the original opinion was wrong; it just means that one person liked that opinion and another did not. If one is to listen to everyone's comments; if a producer is attempting to please everyone—you might just end up with the theatrical equivalent of the lowest-common-denominator. And that, I'm afraid, is what we're getting today; over and over again.

If you take a look at the *Ragtime* advertising campaign of the time—the window card (theatrical poster) for example—you will see a montage of imagery chosen in an attempt to simultaneously visualize several of *Ragtime*'s storylines—scenes which audiences chose as their favorite moments in the show. The result, I'm afraid to say, was a poster/advertising/marketing campaign with little focus, little direction. Indeed, it may have been an honest attempt to appeal to everyone; yet it was clear that most audiences *prior* to seeing the show (after being exposed to the advertising campaign only) were a just bit confused as to what the musical was actually all about.

It was a shame. A brilliant American musical; spectacularly written and staged and designed and acting . . . perhaps doomed from the start. Perhaps it was all those additional marketing dollars Garth requested—on top of an already overly-expensive production—which may have expedited that great musicals premature closing. It's a business, after all. And if a show's weekly operating costs are quite a bit higher than what that same show's maximum weekly revenue might ever be able to be—there is only one way out.

But lessons are not often learned in the theatre. The concept of marketing questionnaires and other forms of audience polling has unfortunately caught on. Radio City Entertainment, for example, has taken on the practice of audience polling with its own seasonal blockbuster *The Radio City Christmas Spectacular* . . . asking audiences which scenes they liked, and which scenes they did not. The hoped-for result, of course, is that when it comes time to update that show, Radio City's creative team will be able to give audiences just what they've asked for. Having been the Executive Producer of that show from 1982 until 1990 [working directly with the show's original creator Robert Jani]; and then again from 2001 through 2003 . . . I'm somewhat afraid to see just what that might be.

"Nothing can please many, and please long, but just representations of general nature."

—William Shakespeare

And so it is today—corporations produce; committees decide.

And because of it, some say New York theatre has become a Broadway of mega-hits only . . . that the more unusual, perhaps more interesting, more daring pieces, wouldn't dare come anywhere near Broadway today. And if true, that's a very sad state for the industry.

Indeed, where have all the leaders gone? There aren't many left these days on the Great White Way. And the shows which have opened the past several seasons have proven that over and over again.

And so, you might ask—are there any producers still willing to take risks? My answer is yes, but I believe those brave men and women are taking their risks elsewhere.

Off-Broadway is seeing a revival of sorts—perhaps a theatrical renaissance not seen since the early 1960s. In an odd sort of way, we appear to be returning to those great experimental days of the theatrical fringe movement. And it's no doubt because the Off-Broadway producing landscape is far less costly and therefore seems a far more practical forum in which to premiere a new musical or dramatic work. Simply put, there's much less to lose.

So today, Off-Broadway is where one just might have the opportunity to see shows one would never be able to see on the Great White Way.

Regional Theatres across America are seeing a renaissance of sorts as well; a great resurgence of interest in new and different works. Non-profit partnerships and alliances of all kinds between commercial producers and the various regional theatre companies appear to be popping up wherever the eye can see. And some of these theatre companies are indeed booming. Seattle Rep, The Gutherie, The Goodman, San Diego Repertory—their reputations for quality is unquestioned. All exist in fertile theatrical geographies, and maintain a solid audience subscription base. Indeed, they've become a perfect environment in which a commercial producer might try out his new production on a smaller scale (lower budget), have a built in audience (subscription series) so all box office concerns are fast done away with. It is an environment which allows the production and creative teams ample time and freedom to work on the show and get it up and running as far away from New York City as possible.

So this has become a win-win situation. The regional non-profit theatre company gets to co-produce an original new work with the hopes of a successful commercial run down the line; the commercial producer utilizes the theatre company's stage and subscription audience to preview creative and production value, and receive quite savvy feedback from an extremely educated audience of first-class theatre-goers. And thus a theatrical marriage is born—perhaps made in heaven. And if the show in fact succeeds, and eventually makes it to the Great White Way, the potential profits are split and everyone is happy.

For those producers who care not for the glamour and glitter of a grand Broadway Opening and are only in it for the money, then mounting a show specifically to tour is indeed the way to go. Touring, it seems, is the true moneymaker.

There are many examples of how touring shows is becoming more and more the marketplace most lucrative. Many shows are produced solely for the touring market—never intending to proceed to Broadway at all; perfectly content to simply bounce from one regional city to another, raking in the dough.

The Music Of Andrew Lloyd Webber; *Joseph and the Amazing Technicolor Dreamcoat*; the recent revival of *Best Little Whorehouse in Texas* starring Ann-Margret; *Some Like It Hot* starring Tony

Curtis. These shows were produced solely to tour. The idea, of course, is that well-produced theatrical shows do extremely well on the road, especially with a star or two's name placed conspicuously above the title. And if those producers are able to keep a show running on the road as long as possible—well then, that could most certainly be their very own pot of gold.

Some producers who have greatly succeeded at mounting such "road-only shows" have been known to say that the *last* place to do a Broadway show these days is on Broadway.

Not one of these shows in question would dare come to Broadway out of sheer fear, of course, that the New York critics would smash them cold; that the money-tap would run dry in an instant. And of course, everyone knows that once a show is panned by the New York critics, it becomes far more difficult then to return it to the road.

Ann-Margret's *The Best Little Whorehouse in Texas* took in $32.6 million on the road its first year—something it could never have achieved in a far more competitive New York marketplace.

Another example—perhaps a bit more interesting, in fact— is *Mama Mia!* When that show first opened in London in 1999 and quickly reached epic word-of-mouth status as *the* show to see, it was clear that the next step for its producers was an attempt to conquer a much larger theatrical marketplace—Broadway and the United States.

But *Mama Mia!* is an unusual type of theatrical product for sure. And its producers were rather uncertain as to how their show would be perceived by the New York critics. So they conjured up an ingenious plan. First take the show to Toronto—a near-US city already proven to have great theatre-arts audience support; then move the show to two cult markets within the United States (Los Angeles and San Francisco) where they believed the show's 1970's camp music style would be supported as well . . . all in an effort to recoup most of the shows production and operating costs before venturing to New York City. With *Mama Mia!* taking-in over $1 million per week in San Francisco alone (not an easy task to say the least, in that very non-theatrical of American cities), they were able to recoup nearly *all* of their production costs prior to their New York bow. So when their curtain finally went up at the Winter Garden Theatre in October 2001, *Mamma Mia!* was completely out of debt. The critical response then would seem far less important to that show's producers. With their investments already paid off, anything they took in at the box office from then on would be theatrical gravy indeed.

X Marks The Spot

One element that has clearly helped make Broadway what it is today is the very controversial changing face of Times Square.

Times Square. Where Broadway and Seventh Avenue intersect, creating the veritable cross-roads of the theatrical world.

Many of you are already aware of the incredible changes that have taken place in New York's historic theatre district over the past ten years. Some have called it the "Disney-fication" of Times Square, as the Disney Corporation was perhaps the one organization most responsible for that area's renaissance. It's cleaner. It's safer. Shops have sprung up in nearly every available space. There's a renewed interest in getting out and walking about. Crime is at its lowest in nearly thirty years; Subway/Metro stations and services have improved, and all of the adult-type entertainments have been relocated to newly re-zoned parts of the city.

A revitalized Times Square has indeed impacted *positively* on Broadway attendance and overall revenue, and made Broadway once again *the* place to go for good, solid, reliable, high quality entertainment—in a safe, clean, family-friendly environment.

Another Circus, Another Show

When producing a show—any show—the first thing a producer must understand is his audience. For whom is he producing the show? Who is the intended target; who might want to buy tickets?

So it's important to consider what the current audience base might be at that particular time in Broadway history. What are the demographics? What are their interests? What are their expectations?

In essence, the Broadway audience is segmented into three rather distinct groups:

· The locals—Manhattan-ites
· The "bridge and tunnel" crowd—those living in the 100-mile radius of New York City, popularly known as the tri-state area
· Tourists

All three of these audience groups are essential to getting a show open, and keeping it up and running for many years.

Manhattan-ites – Seen it. Been there. Done that.

The local population—the theatre crowd, as they are often called—are really quite savvy, or at least they would like to think they are. They see many shows on and off Broadway each year, and have a good understanding of theatrical history overall. They are smart, opinionated, and terribly impatient. Their expectations are really quite high. They want to be the very first to see a new show, and the very first to form a solid verbal opinion. They could be your best ally in opening your show, and they can also be a show's downfall. Unless they are taken quite off guard—

unless they are given quite unusual content in a well-staged production—they could be the very first to kill a show cold. Indeed, negative word of mouth from theatre-savvy Manhattanites is the theatre's worst nightmare. It can prevent a truly fine show from actually getting off the ground. Indeed, it's those up front, rather strong, and quite negative opinions which at times can never really be overcome.

The Bridge and Tunnel Crowd

The BTC is the second audience group to consider, and the mainstay of many a production. They, at least, like to think of themselves as savvy and perhaps just as important as the Manhattan-ites; they strive to show their theatrical knowledge whenever and wherever they can. And most producers believe they can be often-times easily swayed by clever marketing and advertising tactics.

Bob Fosse knew well how to divert an audience's attention. "How can they see with sequins in their eyes . . ." the voice of Billy Flynn sings out in John Kander and Fred Ebb's *Chicago*. And indeed, that's been proven true in many many instances. Making an audience feel they are getting more than what they paid for is an important theatrical illusion which can literally make or break your production. And with the Bridge and Tunnel Crowd, this can be achieved not only through clever staging, but through even more clever marketing techniques as well.

Tourists

International. Domestic. English-speaking; or those not understanding a word. This is by far the most important audience group for most producers' long-term strategy, for they are absolutely essential in order to achieve a long Broadway run. They are a culturally divergent group; and seem to flock to those productions which rely on vibrant visuals in scenic and other special effects.

However with all of their differences in language and cultural likes and dislikes, these audience groups are no doubt citizens of a similar world. And so its important to take a quick look at what might have influenced them over the years; what is influencing them today; indeed, what their expectations might be once they set foot inside a Broadway theatre.

The Arrangement of the Screens

In the United States at the turn of the century, we live in a movie-going world. Cinema is the staple. It's easily accessible, and cleverly priced for the masses. So audiences are quite accustomed to the lavish spectacle they often witness in movie houses worldwide. Sub-consciously or not, theatre audiences today are expecting those same, somewhat impressive, special effects they so often see in films like *Titanic, Matrix II*, and (heaven forbid) *Terminator 114*.

Special effects so common on the silver screen—if transposed to the Broadway stage—create huge production and operational costs, and these often times are quite financially impractical to keeping a show open. From twenty years back or more, producers have tried their best to give audiences such effects. *The Phantom of the Opera, Miss Saigon, Titanic* . . . intelligent lighting systems, haze and smoke and dry ice too; chandeliers and helicopters falling from the flies over the audience, and baby grand pianos sliding across the deck of a glamorous new ocean liner and down into the depths of the sea.

Now none of this should be considered bad theatrics. Indeed, theatrical designers should be congratulated for the many marvels they have been able to achieve in such a limited work space.

But some in the audience have complained that the theatre was becoming more about how much "stuff" you could get onto the stage and less about the story. That it was no longer the playwright's theatre of Williams and Inge and Miller and Ibsen. That it was no longer the director's theatre of Kazan, and Nichols, and Fosse and Bennett. Yes—some have even lamented that it had become the designer's theatre of John Napier and Bob Crowley and Scott Pask, just to name a few.

I personally disagree. I believe design is truly a key element in telling any story. It's only when design is used solely for the sake of great design, that a producer—and the entire production—can get into trouble.

In addition to the influence of the great silver screen, audiences have been impacted by the ubiquitous television sit-com; this, of course, a scenario recognized on both sides of the Atlantic. Audiences today are getting more and more accustomed to very simple story-lines —*Seinfeld, Friends, Frasier, Will and Grace*. Now let there be no doubt that these are funny shows indeed, but there is also not much thinking involved with them either. Viewers aren't really challenged. And because of it, audiences have become far more passive in what might be called their theatre involvement—ironic, it seems, in an age of such great interactivity and new media galore.

Most recently television audiences have been bombarded with the very latest craze—the reality show. *Survivor, Fear Factor, The Bachelor/Bachelorette, Average Joe, The Apprentice, My Big Fat Obnoxious Fiancé*, and perhaps most shocking . . . *Who Wants To Marry My Dad?*

And with the *convenience* of TV/film/video so easily available at the local Blockbuster or by way of your very own in-house Cable TV/Pay-Per-View network or even TiVo®, audiences can have all they want just at their fingertips. And they don't even have to leave the comfort of their homes.

Where Do We Go From Here?

So. What are producers doing about all this?

Film producers and advertisers alike have long ago realized that the greatest profit potential they can ever hope to garner is easily achieved by targeting youth. And Broadway producers—traditionally known to target the more wealthy, perhaps older, social crowds—have only just caught on. So there has been great effort in recent years to attract more young people to Broadway shows. And that effort appears to be paying off . . .

The number of ticket holders under the age of eighteen has more than tripled from 1980 through 2002. In 2003, those under the age of eighteen represented 11.1% of the theatre-going audience, representing 1,267,917 tickets sold.

These statistics appear to show that Broadway just might be reversing the trend of attracting only an older audience. And that's a very good thing. After all . . . in looking ahead . . . if you're trying to encourage a thirty-five-year-old to go to the theatre, you perhaps have a much better chance if that thirty-five-year-old went to the theatre when he was a child.

There might be several possible explanations for the rise in younger theatre-goers on Broadway these days:

- The economy, at least until the late 1990's, was doing quite well. And in late 2003 and early 2004, it seems to be soaring once again
- Many baby-boomers—now in their late 40's and 50's—delayed childbearing, putting many of their children in the five-eighteen age group
- More Broadway shows are suitable to family audiences

And that's the old chicken and the egg-type statistic. Are there more shows appropriate for children and young adults because the audience is larger, or is the audience larger because there are more such shows?

Producers have also begun an aggressive campaign to attract not only younger people to their theatres, but entire families as well. And to this point, they have succeeded.

Broadway "Kid's Night Out"

Broadway "Kids Night Our" is a wonderful outreach campaign, usually available throughout the month of January each year—notoriously the worst month in the Broadway year—whereby one child, accompanied by an adult paying the full ticket price, will be able to attend that same Broadway performance for free. As Martha Stewart would say, this is a very good thing.

Student Discounts

Most Broadway producers are now offering student tickets for many or all of their scheduled performances. Whether it's day-of sale only, or future purchase discounts simply by showing a legitimate high school or university affiliation, students can attend Broadway shows for as little as $20.

Educational Tie-ins

More and more producers are offering educational study programs to schools and other educational institutions. During its historic sixteen-year Broadway run, for example, Cameron Mackintoshes' *Les Miserables* was well marketed to school groups offering them show tickets and an after-performance "meet the cast", in addition to a workbook which allowed students to study the Victor Hugo masterpiece in a truly unique way.

During the 2002-2003 theatrical season, the League of American Theatres and Producers sponsored a report called: "*Who Goes to Broadway: A Demographic Study of the Broadway Audience.*" The results came directly from questionnaires filled out by audience members at various theatres throughout New York.

That study found that:
- the average Broadway theatre-goer is forty-three years old, compared to forty-four in the 2001-2002 season, and forty-two in the 2000-2001 season
- two-thirds of the audience is over thirty-five
- women comprise 63.7% of the audience
- 82.9% of the audience is white
- only 3.8% of the audience is black
- 78% of the theatre-going audience over the age of twenty-five hold a college degree
- the average annual household income is $107,400, compared to $105,000 reported during the 2001-2002 season, and $93,000 in the 2000-2001 season
- 68% of the audience group sees more than one Broadway show per year
- 42% of the audience attended two-to-four Broadway shows per year
- 6% sees fifteen or more shows per year . . . and this cluster of Broadway regulars accounts for 33% of all ticket sales

Another interesting result was that forty-five percent of the Broadway audience during the 2002-2003 seasons was considered to be local—from New York City and its suburbs. Fifty-five percent then were tourists.

The number of Broadway theatre-goers from New York City and its suburbs had increased by more than a million from 1990 – 2003. And this somewhat discounts the belief that Broadway was increasingly attracting an audience of out-of-towners and tourists who are only interested in the big splashy musicals.

Interestingly, the report encouraged producers to market their shows to women—not only because women make up a sizable percentage of the audience, but mostly because they are the ones who decide which shows to see for nearly two-thirds of all ticket sales.

But a truly interesting fact which came out of this report was that Broadway seems to be well attended by those under eighteen years of age, and those over twenty-four. It's the eighteen to twenty-four year old market that's been missing (8.9% of the audience during the 2002-2003 season).

Clearly, producers are juggling three balls at once. Not only do they have to produce a quality show of high production value and content, and market that show aggressively in multiple media, but keep one eye endlessly open for varied audience segments and their very fickle needs and desires too. Indeed, in most people's minds after all, it's a show's box office receipts which truly determine whether or not a producer (and/or his production) is a success.

Inevitably, producers do what they must do. And often times, ground-breaking marketable ideas occur simultaneously throughout the industry. So trends develop, and in hindsight, those trends give us all an excellent view of where we might indeed be headed.

Just what are some of the trends taking over Broadway these days?

There are several production trends which appear to be setting the current landscape on Broadway. Let's take a look at each of them in some detail.

The "New" Golden Age of the American Musical

For years, we've been hearing that the theatre—especially musical theatre—has been dying, if its not already dead. Perhaps "artistically" many feel it may indeed be dead and long buried—but guess what . . . its still here—doing better than ever financially. It's changing perhaps, but still here nonetheless.

And change is good. It's *always* good. Its how we learn, and how we grow.

Producers today are trying everything they can to be as diverse as possible in their programming. And so we're seeing:

- Rock Musicals (*Rent, Hedwig and the Angry Inch* . . .)
- Pop-rock Musicals (*Jeckyll & Hyde, The Civil War, Dance of the Vampires* . . .)
- Classic Musicals (Revivals – *Chicago, Kiss Me Kate, Music Man, Oklahoma!, Into the Wood, Gypsy* . . .)

- Cultural/Ethnic Dramas and Musicals—(*Bombay Dreams, Caroline, or Change* . . .)
- Retrospectives (*Fosse, Putting It Together* . . .)
- Childrens Musicals (*Beauty and the Beast, The Lion King, A Year with Frog and Toad* . . .)
- Teen Musicals (*Footloose* . . .)

In each of these attempts, producers are actively seeking to attract a good deal of repeat business, something not usually a key objective during Broadway's more traditional years.

Take for example the Frank Wildhorn's 1997 musical *Jekyll & Hyde*. For some odd reason, this show garnered a tremendous following. There were groups of people who loved this show so much, some of them had seen it sixty times. A cult following was formed . . . "Jekkies" they were called, in homage to the massive *Star Trek* phenomenon. And their passion for this show, and it's revolving-door star (celebrity) policy, made them return over and over to New York's historic Plymouth Theatre, shelling out serious dollars to the welcoming box office coffers.

Cleverly, *Jekyll & Hyde's* producers quickly identified an opportunity and jumped on to the proverbial bandwagon. They helped give their audience exactly what they wanted by offering special ticket discounting especially for their "Jekkies", as well as backstage visits with the stars, and more. Naturally, the producers wanted to maximize their audience's attachment to their show. It was clear that once an audience got hooked on a production, they would return, over and over again—especially if there was something to entice them even more than the show itself. Such as a new young "star."

So a promising new ticket-selling market was identified—the repeat buyer. And today, this has become a unique new marketing opportunity much sought after by theatrical producers worldwide.

Indeed, cultivating repeat business is not only key to the theatrical industry today, it's essential. And it's not such an easy thing to achieve in the current marketplace where audience's attention-spans are dwindling by the minute, and where ticket pricing has made it even more difficult for an audience to afford such a luxury.

The advent of new and better theatrical facilities in the Broadway theatre district has also helped create a more eager marketplace.

The refurbishment of the aging New Amsterdam Theatre by the Disney Corporation several years ago was so beautifully done, it's worth the price of a ticket alone to see the wonders of that classic auditorium. Simply by having their marvelous production *The Lion King* performed each night in that glorious space has only added to the theatrical pie.

Quite soon after it's opening in 1998, The Ford Center for the Performing Arts—also located on famed 42nd Street—quickly became one of New York's most modern theatres. It's a lavish 1,839-seat auditorium constructed on the site of two classic houses—the Lyric and the Apollo—and incorporates the original architectural elements from both of those theaters, along with state-of-the-art facilities to accommodate grand-scale musicals. Its spacious scale and near perfect views of the stage from most audience locations, has made the theatre-going experience there really quite pleasant.

And as I've already discussed, The Roundabout Theatre Company has done a perfectly fine job of refurbishing the much deteriorating Selwyn Theatre, also on 42nd Street. Debuting as their new American Airlines/Selwyn Theatre, this spectacular yet intimate new space has certainly enhanced the Roundabout's fine theatrical reputation, now finally headquartered in New York's historic theatre district.

The most recent $36 Million redesign and refurbishment of the famed Biltmore Theatre (circa 1925) on West 48th Street by Manhattan Theatre Club is certainly causing many heads to spin. The Biltmore Theatre, once home to such Broadway classics as the 60s Rock Tribal sensation *Hair* and Neil Simon's *Barefoot In The Park*, was torched by arsonists in 1987 and has been dormant ever since. New York Mayor Michael Bloomberg officiated at the Opening Night festivies—October 15, 2003.

Along with the Mayor, standing together on a windswept platform, Barry Grove—The Manhattan Theatre Club's Executive

Producer—said "It was important to rescue it (The Biltmore Theatre) not just because the Manhattan Theatre Club needed to find a Broadway home, but because we need these theatres. They are the largest concentration of theatrical real estate in the world, they anchor the tourism economy of New York City, and their plays and musicals entertain us and teach us about our lives."

Debra A Waxman, MTC's Director of marketing told Playbill On-Line that day "I think they've done a fabulous job. [They] preserved the feeling that you're in a historically landmarked space when you're in the auditorium, but you also get the sense that there's nothing old about it."

Not to be ignored is the re-opening of a new complex of theatres on West 42nd Street's famed "Theatre Row" including several new performance facilities for Playwright's Horizons, as well as the new Little Shubert Theatre—a spanking new Off-Broadway facility, just down the block.

There's also a new Off-Broadway theatre complex of theatres currently in construction just to the north on West 50th Street— a former cinema complex once located there is now being transformed into newly designed theatrical facilities by Dodger Theatricals.

Tell Me On A Sunday

It appears that after many seasons to the contrary, we are perhaps just beginning to see that more shows might indeed be critic proof. Indeed, Frank Rich—the celebrated "butcher of Broadway"—is gone; sadly though, still proselytizing his personal artistic opinions and political leanings on *The New York Times'* Op-Ed Page—Sunday Edition, but gone from *officially* covering theatre nonetheless. And in one man's opinion, that's a very good thing. For Mr. Rich—with all his great intelligence and writing skills; with all his pomp and circumstance aside—no doubt helped to change the theatrical landscape for the worse. By having the power and therefore the ability to close a new show with the stroke of his pen, he no doubt paved the way for the current no-risk-taking landscape we are all currently experiencing.

No producer wants to risk his personal and financial investment and therefore his potential future profits on the word of a single critic. Mr. Rich indeed had that power, and often times used it more, in my opinion, to promote himself and his own personal career, than to truly assess the production then playing before him and to advise future audiences just what was in store. Indeed, one who can't create—or can't produce, for that matter—can yet so easily criticize.

So with that one great voice gone forever from the brilliance of Broadway's lights, more and more shows do seem to be able to create a market for themselves and just eke out a run, much to the support of their own personal fans. We are seeing more and more audiences beginning to make choices for themselves that not too long ago they would let the critics—and perhaps more specifically Mr. Rich—make on their behalf.

Trend #1 — The Broadway Show, yet again

It seems that all we've been seeing these last years on Broadway is an endless stream of revivals. Just look at an abbreviated list:

- *Oklahoma*
- *Into the Woods*
- *Kiss Me Kate*
- *Chicago*
- *Cabaret*
- *The Music Man*

- *I'm Not Rappaport*
- *The Elephant Man*
- *Private Lives*
- *Guys and Dolls*
- *The Sound of Music*
- *How to Succeed in Business Without Really Trying*
- *Nine*
- *Man of La Mancha*
- *Gypsy*
- *Long Days Journey Into Night*
- *A Day in the Death of Joe Egg*
- *The Rocky Horror Show*
- *42nd Street*
- *Wonderful Town*
- *Cat On A Hot Tin Roof*
- *Fiddler on the Roof*
- *Dreamgirls*
- *La Cage aux Folles*
- *Camelot*

And why, you might ask? Little Risk!

Producers are businessmen, after all; they cannot be fools. They understand the all-too-fickle and unpredictable marketplace we're in today, and realize that the less risk they can take, the better off they (and their investors, or course) will be.

And so we end up with a stream of endless revivals with, their producers hope, a built-in following. Who can argue with that? No one, except perhaps an audience interested in and eager for great new theatrical works.

While it's important to pay tribute to the great shows of the past . . . when we give in to romanticizing *only* Broadway's bygone years, we do risk missing out on the vitality playing out right before our eyes. And that would be a shame, indeed.

Trend #2 — Theatre Goes to the Movies

Without a doubt, Broadway has certainly been going to the movies these past few seasons—and it's a trend which I believe will continue well on into the future.

It's an easy strategy, after all. A producer purchases the rights to a successful film, and cleverly transforms that screenplay into a new stage play or musical.

Several years ago, this trend began as only a trickle. I'm talking about such shows as:

- *Victoria/Victoria*
- *La Cage Aux Folles*
- *Meet Me in St. Louis*
- *Singing in the Rain*
- *Footloose*
- *Whistle Down the Wind*
- *Kiss Of The Spider Woman*

What's interesting of course is that this trend seems to be the reverse of what historically has been the Broadway-to-film model . . . for both plays and musicals.

In it's heyday—perhaps the 1950s-1960s—a script was first produced on Broadway; that was its start. And only if that show received universal acclaim, would it soon be transferred to the great silver screen.

Let's look at just a brief listing of stage to film productions over the years which illustrate this trend:

Musicals
- *My Fair Lady*
- *Hello Dolly*
- *West Side Story*
- *Sweet Charity*
- *Guys and Dolls*
- *South Pacific*
- *Mame*
- *The Sound of Music*

Dramas/Plays

- *Whose Afraid of Virginia Woolf*
- *Cat On A Hot Tin Roof*
- *Night of the Iguana*
- *A Streetcar Named Desire*

All of these shows first opened on Broadway; first succeeded on Broadway; then and only then they were able to transfer to film, and on to national and international success at the box office.

Today, however, more and more producers are seeing the value in properties which have already succeeded in film—reworking them, and transporting them to the stage.

Once again, the feeling is that there is already a built-in audience for these storylines, it's a product the public already knows (so there's little or no risk), and it offers excellent public relations and marketing opportunities as well.

Creatively, this is an interesting process to observe. Because it's not as easy a task to do as one would think.

Take a piece like *Footloose*, for example—not a musical film at all when it was first released in 1984, although there were clearly songs in the film which were used to highlight and underscore the action. And those songs did indeed have great success on the pop charts.

So the writers of *Footloose—The Musical* had an interesting dilemma in front of them. They knew they had to include all the music made popular on the pop charts in their new stage musical; their potential new audience would certainly expect that. But they wouldn't be able to use those songs as underscore as they appeared in the film; they had to work them directly into the script. They now had to give those songs to the various characters to sing live onstage, in order to tell their story clearly and more succinctly.

And they did a marvelous job. At least in my opinion they did. I'm sure that was not an easy thing to pull off.

Over the last several seasons—including the 2003-2004 Broadway season—just some of the shows which follow this film-to-stage musical trend . . . shows which have either already opened, or are planning to open (on both sides of the Atlantic) are:

- *The Full Monty*
- *The Producers*
- *The Witches of Eastwick*
- *Hairspray*
- *Peggy Sue Got Married*
- *Thoroughly Modern Millie*
- *The Sweet Smell of Success*
- *Heaven Can Wait*
- *Chitty Chitty Bang Bang*
- *Dance of the Vampires (Roman Polanski)*

- *Moonstruck*
- *Dead Man Walking*
- *Batman* '
- *Mary Poppins*
- *An American in Paris*
- *The Night They Raided Minskys*
- *The Pink Panther*
- *Bladerunner*
- *Edward Scissorhands*

The great irony of course is that despite the amazing success of Miramax Film's *Chicago*; and of course Baz Lurman's *Moulin Rouge;* and perhaps even Madonna's *Evita* of 1996—few people seem to care about film musicals these days. And perhaps even more importantly, few movie studios care about film musicals these days; they seem quite leery about making such an investment.

Yet it appears more and more people want to see a new musical based on an already popular film.

After all, it took almost twenty-seven years to get *Chicago* made into a film. It took nearly twenty years for *Evita*, even with Madonna's name attached to the project. And Andrew Lloyd Webber's *The Phantom of the Opera* film has been kicking around Hollywood for years . . . and has only recently begun filming in England and the environs of Paris.

So what, if any, are some of the upcoming film musical projects still on the boards? Still celebrating the massive success of their spectacular *Chicago*, Miramax has announced they have just obtained the film rights to Frank Loesser and Abe Burrows's *Guys and Dolls,* and Stephen Schwartz and Roger O. Hirson's *Pippin.*

And Andrew Lloyd Webber and Ben Elton's *The Beautiful Game* is currently slated as a future movie musical as well.

We'll soon see if indeed any of these proposed musical film projects ever do see the light of day.

Trend #3 Karaoke Conquers Broadway

This is perhaps the most frightening trend of them all. It could be called "star power." And that's, of course, star with a *small* "s". In fact, let's simply go back to calling them celebrities rather than stars.

Once again, this is the practice of casting popular celebrities in the leads of new or revived Broadway musicals or plays, whether or not that celebrity has the talent or even the ability to handle the role. They are cast simply because they are well known to an audience. They are there to guarantee solid box office revenues. And we will soon see, it's become clear that only television and film stars have become the Broadway stars of today.

In recent years, we've seen the leads in Broadway shows taken by a host of characters—all television and sitcom stars I might add:

- Kelsey Grammer (*Macbeth*)
- Cheryl Ladd (*Annie Get Your Gun*)
- David Hasselloff (*Jekyll & Hyde*)
- Eric McCormick (*The Music Man*)

And music /pop stars are not immune to this trend either:

- Ricky Martin (*Les Miserables* and *The Boy from Oz*)
- Deborah Gibson (*Beauty and the Beast* and *Les Miserables*)
- Toni Braxton (Disney's *Beauty and the Beast*; Disney's *Aida*)
- Rheba McEntyre (*Annie Get Your Gun*)
- Jon Secada (*Cabaret*)

And when—in the summer of 2002—Barry and Fran Weissler cast the film star Melanie Griffith as Roxie Hart in their New York production of *Chicago*, I think everyone in the industry simply threw up their hands in utter frustration. The morning after she opened, the front page of *The New York Daily News* boasted a huge photograph of the glamorous Ms. Griffith in typical Roxie garb—with the giant headline "She Can't Sing Dance or Act . . . But She's a Star!" And on top of it all, she received glowing notices for her performance. Amazing. A non-singing/non-dancing star of a Broadway musical!

So clearly, the image of the great Broadway star has changed. Not too long ago, the term "Broadway star" meant an actor with amazing skills; a highly professional stage performer—one easily capable of making an audience *feel* something. At times, words were not even required—it simply took an actor's walking onto the stage for most in the audience to know they were then in the presence of someone special; and that something truly magical was about to happen.

Take Angela Landsbury, for example. Most would agree she's an amazing stage performer with numerous Tony and other awards to reflect her legendary performances in such stage classics as *Mame*, *Dear World*, *Gypsy*; and of course for Stephen Sondheim's masterpiece *Sweeney Todd*. Yet ironically, she's perhaps more valuable to a producer today for her long-running stint as Jessica Fletcher in *Murder, She Wrote*, than for all her stellar turns on the great stages of the world.

A few seasons back, the popular American comedienne Rosie O'Donnell stepped into the lead of the financially struggling and critically-dissed Broadway musical *Seussical* for a limited run. And even though she was ostensibly portraying the Cat in the Hat, she was actually playing herself—the then popular talk-show host, sometime actress and stand-up comic.

However talented Ms. O'Donnell might be—and she is quite amusing at times—she's a woman who many feel can't sing, dance, or act . . . not unlike Ms. Griffith. Yet she was starring in a Broadway show. And in *Seussical,* no less—in my opinion, perhaps one of the finest new American musicals in years.

And even more frightening than that . . . she was saving a Broadway show.

Just her presence alone increased awareness and overall ticket sales. It was said that box office receipts increased over two hundred thousand dollars the very first day Rosie O'Donnell's name was announced.

In December 2003, the producer's of *The Boy From Oz* announced that their show would go on hiatus while it's star—Hugh Jackman—went off on holiday. Whatever happened to old show business adage "the show must go on?" It just proves, unfortunately, that even the show's producers believe *The Boy From Oz* just might not be worth their $101.25 ticket price without the presence of their famous film-star lead.

Trend #4 The *Graying* of the Great White Way . . .

I doubt anyone could describe Broadway's most recent seasons as fresh or daring or adventurous. But when you look at those seasons in detail, you will clearly see a palette of work from some truly amazing Broadway veterans:

- Bea Arthur (*Bea Arthur on Broadway*) 78
- Elaine Stritch (*Elaine Stritch At Liberty*) 76
- Barbara Cook 74
- Edward Albee (*The Goat*) 73
- Neil Simon (*45 Seconds From Broadway*) 74
- Stephen Sondheim (*Into the Woods*) 71
- Arthur Miller 86 (*Crucible/The Man Who Had All The Luck*)

On the one hand, it was a unique opportunity for a younger audience to see the work of some of these fine artists who have helped to give Broadway the reputation it has had and maintained over the years.

On the other hand, it illustrates a great hidden fear chilling the Broadway industry of late—the continued concerns about the advanced aging of the potential Broadway audience, and the unwillingness of Broadway to take a chance on anything but the familiar.

It also could illustrate the plaguing inability of Broadway to attract and keep young innovative playwrights writing for the stage.

Arthur Miller—whose very first Broadway play *The Man Who Had All The Luck* opened in 1944 and closed after only four performances—recently said:

"these days, Broadway has little time for serious new plays by young writers. In addition" he said, "the significance of the theatre in society has been greatly reduced, so it's more difficult for a writer to get excited about writing for the stage."

"The significance of the theatre in society has been greatly reduced . . ."

How sad, if true.

Trend #5 Behind The Music

Whatever could a Detroit soul singer, a country boy, and a hippie possibly have in common?

A lot . . . based on this successful new trend of creating "pop icon" biographical musicals.

It all began perhaps back in the 70's and 80's with the great success of Fat's Waller's *Ain't Misbehavin'* and Duke Ellington's *Sophisticated Ladies*.

In the 1990's we saw a massive interest in this type of production with the international sensation *The Who's Tommy*.

Followed soon after by the long running Leiber and Stoller revue *Smokey Joe's Café*.

And today? Just some of the productions which follow this "Behind the Music" phenomenon are:

- *The Jackie Wilson Story*
- *Hank Williams: Lost Highway*
- *Dream a Little Dream* — The Mamas and the Papas Musical
- *Love, Janis* — The Janis Joplin Musical
- *Stand By Your Man* — the Tammy Wynette Musical
- *Mack The Knife* — The Bobby Darrin Musical
- *The Rat Pack* — The Musical (Frank, Dean, and Sammy)
- *The Boy from Oz* — The Peter Allen Musical
- *All Shook Up* — The Elvis Presley Musical
- *Sinatra* — The Frank Sinatra Musical
- *Tonight's The Night* — The Rod Stewart Musical
- *Be My Love*—The Mario Lanza Musical
- A recently announced—currently untitled—John Lennon musical

All these shows, of course, following closely in the steps of the highly successful *Mamma Mia!* (The Abba Musical), *Taboo* (The Boy George/Culture Club Musical), and *Movin' Out* (The Billy Joel Musical)

Again . . . it's music everyone knows. It's characters the audience might already be familiar with. And it's far less of a risk than producing something new and original.

Trend #6 The *new* British Invasion

If one's looks closely at the creative teams making up some of the newest productions on Broadway these days, we're seeing that more and more of the new/or revived musicals are being staged by British directors, not American directors.

- · *Follies* (Revival) — Matthew Warchus
- · *Cabaret* (Revival) — Sam Mendes
- · *Gypsy* (Revival) — Sam Mendes
- · *Man of La Mancha* (Revival) — Jonathan Kent
- · *Oklahoma* (Revival) — Trevor Nunn
- · *Nine* (Revival) — David Leveaux
- · *Sweet Charity* (Revival) — Timothy Sheader
- · *Fiddler on the Roof* (Revival) — David Leveaux

Producer's today are always eager to find new and interesting marketing hooks. They have no choice. If you're going to produce nothing but revivals (which is most of what we're seeing these days), you'd better have something special

The British—both actors and directors—have always held a valiant theatrical prestige here in the colonies. And in fact they do indeed bring a certain freshness to their stage work not necessarily seen in American theatre today. And so, I believe this is a trend we will be seeing more and more of in the coming seasons.

Trend #7 A Hop, Skip, and a Jump

Yes indeed, that dancing phenomenon colloquially called hip-hop has jumped head first onto the stage. We first saw this trend a few years back with shows such as *"Bring in 'Da Noise, Bring in 'Da Funk"* and *"The Bomb-itty of Errors"* as it funked-up the stage in a small warehouse in New York's Greenwich Village before traveling the Atlantic to open in London's West End. But over the last two seasons, we've seen hip-hop shows having a more consistent presence, both in New York and in London.

Russell Simmons' "Def Poetry Jam on Broadway" took home a Tony Award in 2003 as Best Special Theatrical Event.

Will Power's one-man show of record-scratching and free-styling called *Flow*—co-produced by NY Theatre Workshop—had a solid run Off-Broadway this past season.

And in London . . . *"Da Boyz"* an urban reincarnation of the Rodgers and Hart classic *"The Boys from Syracuse"* closed in late summer 2003 after many successful weeks at the Theatre Royal, Stratford East.

DJ Excalibah (who transformed *The Boys from Syracuse* score to a garage, R&B, basement, hip-hop sound) recently said—"the only way to gain the interest of these young people is to give them stuff they want to listen to on the radio and in their houses" . . .

But is the same crowd that pays to see Vanessa Redgrave as enthused about Jay-Z? I wonder. Obviously, the new young producers who are currently bringing such shows to the legitimate stage are targeting a potentially untapped market—ticket-buyers with a passion for hip/hop; those who perhaps had previously never thought of buying a ticket to a theatrical performance either on Broadway or in London's West End. Those producers are no doubt hoping that with the introduction of this unique music style, this potential new audience will be drawn to seeing their hip/hop idol live—in a theatrical—on the great stages of the world. And a potential new marketplace for producers might indeed be born.

However the uneven financial performance of these shows to date suggest that the answer is still uncertain as to whether or not these shows will succeed—whether or not this trend will continue—and perhaps constitute a new stage musical genre as well.

Day By Day

In order to better understand the theatrical landscape at the start of this new century, I think it's best to look at some statistics.

During the 2001–2002 Broadway season, a total of thirty-three shows opened on Broadway, compared to:

- thirty-eight shows in the 1999-00 season
- twenty-eight shows in the 1990-91 season
- fifty shows in the 1982-83 season
- sixty-seven shows in the 1980-81 season

Of those thirty-three shows—sixteen were musicals and seventeen dramas/comedies. And only two are stilling running at the time of this writing:

- *Mamma Mia!*
- *Thoroughly Modern Millie*

Thirty-one then, of the thirty-three shows which opened in the 2001-2002 Broadway season were considered "flops" and resulted in total loss to investors.

At the completion of the 2002-2003 Broadway season, only one production is considered to be a guaranteed "hit" and that's of course *Hairspray*.

September 11, 2001

The impact September 11, 2001 had on Broadway was devastating. Clearly, not only did tourism stop cold in New York that day, but New Yorkers stopped cold as well. None of us wanted to do much of anything.

As I stood on Seventh Avenue that crisp early-autumn morning looking south to the burning towers of the World Trade Center, I instinctively knew that the world would never—could never—be the same.

The violent events of that fateful day instantly precipitated a drop in tourism world-wide. And naturally, this affected not only the overall mood, but the geographic composition of the Broadway audience.

Within days of the September 11th attacks, five Broadway shows had closed and several—including such contemporary "classics" as *The Phantom of the Opera* and *Les Miserables*—had been so hard hit, that they were on the verge of closing as well. It is well known that such shows—having succeeded on Broadway for double-digit years—are mainly kept alive by tourists. And there were no tourists to be had.

Several producers sought and received financial concessions from the various theatrical unions in order to support operating costs and keep their shows open—this, in an effort to get through what they hoped would be just a temporary difficult period. But it was not.

Then New York City Mayor Rudolph Giuliani and his administrative government quickly came to the rescue. The Mayor realized the importance the theatre as an institution—and the arts in general—had not only on rebuilding New York's damaged economy, but its spirit as well. In a press conference shortly after the attacks, the mayor said "as long as Broadway's stages are dark, the city itself will look dark to all the world." And so he and his team led the campaign by urging all New Yorkers not to stay at home—to get out, enjoy a dinner, see a show.

The city purchased nearly $2 million worth of Broadway theatre tickets that week to help get the industry back on its feet; they donated those tickets to the families of the rescue workers tied to their dreadful tasks down at the already infamous Ground Zero.

By the end of the 2001-2002 season, the percentage of domestic tourism in Broadway theatres did return to pre-September 11th levels. However, the percentage of international tourists finished the season at only 6%—up slightly from the previous year but still below its usual 10% mark.

Today, nearly two and a half years later, Broadway appears to have bounced back well—far better, in fact, than any of us thought possible. Thanks to solid support from fellow New Yorkers who know well how important the Broadway theatre is to the image and the spirit of their own great city.

Nonetheless, the future of Broadway—and the way Broadway business is conducted—has been changed forever. Producers learned quickly that day how circumstances can change in an instant. And how with those changing circumstances must come a dynamic change in strategy. Most obvious to note was just how much the long-running productions depended on tourists to keep their doors open. And when that flow of tourism stops cold, abruptly, as it did on that tragic September morning, there might be little left to take its place.

And audiences too learned a lesson that day. They no longer seem to purchase tickets far in advance—a practice producers have always taken for granted. You see, having large sums of money in a show's coffers does indeed make producers feel confident. However suddenly experiencing first-hand how the ticket-buying public has changed its traditional ticket-purchasing habits—buying more short-term—has now made the producing process far more difficult; the speculation on whether or not to keep a show open, far more iffy. Without such a financial cushion, producers might be far more skeptical about keeping a new show open should its reviews be poor to mixed.

Clearly, the entire landscape has changed, and decisions are now made accordingly.

And so producers are feeling their way through this very uncertain time, as best they can.

Greenwich Village Follies

As The New York Times' columnist Bruce Weber so aptly stated in his Critic's Notebook dated July 2, 2003—"Everybody knows what a crapshoot Broadway is. You can't make a living, but you can make a killing."

Indeed, Broadway may be a tough business, but it still brings in the dough. In 2003, Broadway grossed over $730 million, according to the latest figures from The League of American Theatres and Producers. Not so shabby a sum.

But keep in mind—the increased gross revenue numbers we are seeing these days has as much to do with higher ticket prices (an average increase of 5.5 percent over the last year) as it does with attendance, which again dipped slightly from last year.

Shows open and close on Broadway these days in the blink of an eye. But those shows are not the only ones in which Broadway "angels" might lose their entire investment. Even shows which appear to be doing well—those running for long periods of time—can, in fact, just be breaking even; earning just enough to keep the doors open. So although it might appear to the public that a show is successful merely because it has been open a while and is therefore apparently doing well, total investments in such shows are lost all the time.

And with the massive costs of Broadway shows increasing more and more, those lost investments can indeed seem quite considerable.

But a bit more out of the spotlight, one might find that the theatre I still alive and well, and living just a bit Off-Broadway.

When Cole Porter first opened his successful musical revue *Greenwich Village Follies of 1924*, he couldn't have realized the tremendous impact Off-Broadway would one day have on the theatre community as a whole.

It can certainly be argued that Off-Broadway is perhaps the country's most artistically influential and culturally diverse theatrical community. On any given day, one can find literally dozens of productions playing through the city.

But is Off-Broadway the theatre's promise for the future?

First off . . . some basic facts.

I am often asked what exactly is the difference between a Broadway show and an Off-Broadway Show? The answer, in fact, is actually determined by the size of the house (the theatre) in which a particular show plays. So, for the sake of this argument, let's just say that a Broadway Show is any show which plays in a theatre boasting a capacity of five hundred seats or more. Anything below that would be considered Off-Broadway, although theatres with a capacity below one hundred seats are often given Off-Off-Broadway status. And that's a whole different story.

From many viewpoints, the 2002-2003 Off-Broadway season truly teemed with invention. One would first jump to the conclusion that it all makes sense; that it simply costs less to produce Off-Broadway, therefore the risks are smaller and so the fund-raising is less onerous. It seems logical then that more and more producers would want to flock to the Off-Broadway arena in which to develop their productions.

But that's not necessarily the case. In comparison to Broadway budgets, those for an Off-Broadway show might at first seem more reasonable, more practical. That season's Off-

Broadway production of Jack Dalgleish's *Zanna Don't* for example cost over $1 million to mount, whereas that same season's Broadway production of Baz Lurman's *La Bohème* cost ten times that.

But one must consider the scale of the whole; the size of the houses in which each show will play, and therefore the amount of possible potential revenue there might be.

Most Broadway musicals these days have weekly break-even points set at around five hundred thousand dollars or more; while those Off-Broadway can be as little as sixty thousand dollars (as in the case of Dalgleish's *Zanna Don't*).

But with the potential capacity of taking in over one million dollars a week in a 1,000-seat Broadway theatre, and only $127,000 in a 287-seat Off-Broadway theatre, one can easily see the production concerns and the downside of producing Off-Broadway.

Yet what seems the bigger potential just might also mean the bigger the loss. And so it seems that we are still finding more producers (and writers and directors too) far more willing to take a creative chance Off-Broadway on something far more interesting—far more thrilling—than one would ever take on Broadway today. Even though the potential profits are far less.

In his article, Bruce Webber mentioned twenty-six stunning new shows which opened Off-Broadway during the 2002-2003 season . . . in particular five new musicals (including *Zanna Don't*, *Betty Rules*, and *Hank Williams—Lost Highway*), fifteen new plays (including *Writer's Block*, *I Am My Own Wife*, *Stone Cold Dead Serious*, and *The Last Sunday In June*), and seven revivals (including *Valparaiso*, *Talking Heads*, and *High Priest of California*) . . . most of which were lost to many New Yorkers and definitely to most tourists as well. And so most of those shows—if not all of them—closed silently, without a whisper.

Perhaps because of the great public relations push after September 11th to focus audiences on the treasures of Broadway alone . . . perhaps because of the stagnant economy as well . . . perhaps because Off-Broadway shows simply do not get the same high profile in the media that Broadway shows have the potential of getting . . . and perhaps because a ticket to see an Off-Broadway show can easily be as much as $76.25 (*Fame—The Musical*)— Off-Broadway has perhaps suffered more than Broadway itself.

Yet it still has much to offer. Some refer to Off-Broadway as New York's best-kept theatrical secret. It would be a tragedy if only the die-hard fans who already know what treasures exist there are getting the opportunity to see some of New York's finest theatrical experiences.

So the glass-half-empty interpretation of all this is that new plays and musicals are doomed . . . and that even good work produced in theatres with a reduced risk factor is not being supported by the public; that there's no sufficient audience.

I prefer to subscribe to the glass-half-full interpretation: isn't it amazing how much good theatre is being produced under such economic constraints? Artists do, in fact, perform beautifully under duress.

For all their moaning, however, I think producers are essentially optimists and believers . . . with a persistent outlook that there are more worthy shows out there than places to put them. Otherwise, how would you explain the current construction trend of several new Off-Broadway theatres?

- The Little Shubert Theatre on 42nd Street
- 50th Street Theatre Complex (The Dodgers Theatricals, Inc.)
- West 37th Street Theatre Complex (Alan Schuster)

"Clearly, optimism is a necessity in this business" the successful Off-Broadway producer Marc Routh recently said to Bruce Webber of *The New York Times*. Mr. Routh's last Off-Broadway venture was a three-character play by Israel Horovitz called *My Old Lady* that cost $900,000 to produce at the Promenade Theatre and never earned it back. "Otherwise" he continued "you just want to shoot yourself."

My message here . . . just don't simply look at the Broadway rosters. Take a good hard look Off-Broadway—and sometimes even Off-Off Broadway—to experience some truly wonderful theatre.

Although when one sees productions like the recently announced *Cookin'*—a long-running South Korean show which features four Asian chefs given the task of preparing an entire wedding banquet in just one hour; using kitchen utensils to create infectious rhythms and heart-pounding samulnori drumming— slated for Off-Broadway's beautiful Minetta Lane Theatre in 2004, one just has to wonder if the creative decline of Off-Broadway isn't far behind.

Tickets, Please!

Not too long ago, a friend was interested in purchasing tickets for the latest Broadway musical, only just announced in that Sunday's *New York Times*. The box office, the advertisement said, would open at 10.00AM the following day.

So off went my friend, early that morning, to be the very first on line; to have his pick of the very finest tickets available.

You can only imagine his surprise when—although being first in line—the box office manager told him that most of the good orchestra seats were already sold out for the next three months.

The lesson to be learned here is that no matter what the advertisements might say, many of the finest seats in the house might already be sold or pulled off-sale by the time the box office first opens it's doors.

Nonetheless, one should always try to obtain the finest seats available. After all, if you're going to invest $105 per ticket, you should be perfectly sure the location of that seat is the very best it could possibly be.

Today, there are various ways of obtaining tickets to Broadway and Off-Broadway shows. And I'd like to discuss a few of the most reliable ways here:

Direct from the Box Office

Personally, I prefer to purchase my theatre tickets directly from the box office. I prefer the person-to-person/face-to-face communication; it always helps, particularly if there is a problem or if I'm trying to purchase tickets for a popular show with little advance notice. If you can find a way to bond with the box office representative, they can be surprisingly helpful. And the added bonus . . . there is no service charge.

The Times Square Visitor's Center

Located in the beautifully restored landmark Embassy Movie Theatre at 1560 Broadway between 46th and 47th Streets, you will find the Times Square Visitor's Center. Since opening it's doors in September 1998 the Times Square Visitor's Center has consistently welcomed over one million tourists per year. The facility is open from 8.00AM to 8.00PM daily. And in addition to offering same day and advance tickets to Broadway shows, tourists can also purchase New York City tours and MTA Metro-Cards, as well as being offered the services of a full-service US Post Office, and perhaps the only public and handicapped-accessible bathrooms in the city.

Hotel Desk. Concierge.

Most luxury hotels in New York City will offer the services of a concierge eager to help with various guest requests. They will happily arrange the purchase of tickets for all the Broadway shows a guest might want to see, including those sometimes deemed hard-to-get. But one gets nothing for nothing, so be prepared to pay a fairly high service charge, or perhaps exorbitant prices for tickets to the hit of the season.

Ticket Agencies

There are several ticket agencies in New York City. They all work similarly, enforcing similar services fees. Here is just a list of some of them, although I am able to endorse none of them.

- Prestige Entertainment—1 800 243-8849
- Applause Theatre and Entertainment Service, Inc.— 1 212 967-5600
- Tickets Now—1 800 927-2770
- The Keith Prowse Ticket Agency—1 800 669-8687

Telephone/Website Agencies

Telephone tickets agencies have been common on Broadway for several years. Some times, I've used them and they've worked perfectly fine. But I have to admit that more and more, I find purchasing tickets via the Internet not only a great convenience, but a great way to go. Whether it's Ticketmaster or Telecharge, you will find an extremely user-friendly interface on their websites which allows you to view the location of the available seats before you actually make the purchase. Tickets will be mailed to you should time allow; or they can be picked up directly at the box office at show time. Check it out; it really is easy to do. Tickets are sold at face value, plus a service charge—currently $6.00 per ticket—and a handling fee of $2.50.

You might want to check out the Broadway.com and Playbill.com websites as well. Each of their sites offer ticket purchasing opportunities, and quite often at rather impressive discounts.

TKTS @ Duffy Square

Perhaps the most famous location in New York City to purchase tickets is the TKTS Booth at Duffy Square (West 47th Street between Broadway and Seventh Avenue). You can't miss it . . . its a large tent-like structure with a giant TKTS logo printed in bright red paint on all sides. But most identifiable are the lengthy lines of hopeful theatre-goers, eagerly awaiting their ticket purchase.

The TKTS Booth offers "day of" performance tickets only at 25% to 75% off the face-value of the ticket plus a modest service charge. Transactions are cash only (no credit cards are accepted).

For those unwilling to withstand the long lines, you might like to know that there is a second (perhaps less visible) TKTS Booth. It was originally located at the World Trade Center; needless to say, it is no longer there. It re-opened however in late in 2002 in a new location on John and Front Streets in downtown Manhattan. Perhaps the uptown location might offer a better choice of shows, but the downtown TKTS Booth is known for being far less crowded, in addition to offering tickets for next day matinees as well.

The HIT SHOW Club

Perhaps better known as two-fers . . . you might have seen these coupons stacked up at most cash registers throughout the city, and not have known what they were. Each coupon is imprinted for a specific show, offering discounts which vary in percentage and dates of availability. Simply take the coupon directly to the box office and redeem them for the show of your choice. It really couldn't be easier.

CARE TIX . . .

For those socially conscious ticket buyers, you might want to call Broadway Cares/Equity Fights AIDS at 212 974-7500. All proceeds from ticket purchases (tickets are sold at face value, plus a somewhat hefty service charge) will go to help fight that devastating disease which has so changed our world.

HOUSE SEATS

All Broadway producers hold a selection of the finest seats available for each show for the industry. Many of those seats— called House Seats—are contractually given to the show's administrative and creative teams (producer, director, choreographer, the various designers, etc.). This block of tickets is not available for public purchase.

However, if these tickets are not used or claimed by 72-hours prior to a particular performance, they are usually released to the box office for open sale.

So if you know the specific date you'd like to see a particular show—even if that show happens to be the hit of the season—and you're able to be the very first patron at the box office window three days prior to the date you'd like to attend, you just might be able to purchase some of those newly-released house seats, obtaining perhaps some of the best seats in the house.

Off With Their Heads . . .

And lastly, a quick word about scalpers. To put it simply— it's illegal. Don't do it. Don't be a part of it.

Nonetheless, it's everywhere. So be wary when someone approaches you on the street with a handful of tickets.

We are now in an age of computerized ticketing, and computerized tickets are quite easy to counterfeit. Please remember— Broadway theatres will *not* honor counterfeit tickets. So be careful.

For those of you who want the simple facts—

The current New York State law includes a price cap of $5 or 10 percent of the base price of the ticket, plus taxes. For example—a $20 ticket could not be resold for more than $25.

The measure also includes the following protections for consumers:

(a) Each ticket must have its established price printed on its face
(b) Seller must post a price list and provision a receipt upon a purchaser's request
(c) Seller must post its operating license or certificate

For those readers who want to fully understand the depths of the ticket scalping problem, please see Appendix A (which follows at the end of this book) for the full Executive

Summary from New York State Attorney General Eliot Spitzer regarding ticket scalping in New York. The report is quite extensive, and will allow you to understand the great depths this problem poses for producers and theatre-goers alike.

The Broadway Show—Some Statistics

To understand the "state of the art" on Broadway these last years and how well it's been doing, it's perhaps best to take a quick snapshot in time. So let's do just that. Let's take a look at what types of shows were "on the boards" during one particular week, and how well those shows did. So for the purposes of this discussion then, let's say we focus in on the week ending December 14, 2003—the time of this writing

We'll also take a look at the Broadway Box Office Grosses from that same week. This should give us a great overview as to just how healthy the industry really is.

So—we'll look at Broadway Week # 30. Week Ending December 14, 2003

There were thirty-two shows playing on Broadway that week—twenty-three musicals and nine dramas or comedies. And that further breaks down to fourteen new/original works, ten revivals of classic Broadway productions (Trend #1), five "film-to-stage" transfers (Trend #2), and three pop idol musical bios (Trend #5).

And how did those shows do? Let's take a look at the Top Ten Broadway Shows for the week ending December 14, 2003 by theatre capacity:

The Top Ten Broadway Shows	Theatre Capacity
#1 *Mama Mia!*	101.1%
#2 Disney's *The Lion King*	101.0%
#3 *Hairspray*	99%
#4 *Henry IV*	96%
#5 *Wicked*	95%
#6 *The Boy from Oz*	94%
#7 *Chicago*	89%
#8 *Cat On A Hot Tin Roof*	87%
#9 *Never Gonna Dance*	85%
#10 *Wonderful Town*	84%

The Top Ten was comprised of eight musicals (two of which were revivals (Trend #1); one a film-to-stage transfer (Trend #2); and one a pop musical "bio" (Trend #5) and two dramas (both of which were revivals).

You might be surprised to see that the 2003 Tony Award Winner "Best Play"—*Take Me Out* by Richard Greenberg, perhaps the finest American play to land on Broadway in years—was not in the Top Ten. It grossed only $176,836 out of a potential $495,036. The show sold at 43% of capacity that week; well below it's weekly break-even point. And has already posted its closing notice for early January 2004.

The 2002 Tony Award Winner "Best Musical"—*Thoroughly Modern Millie*—was not in the Top Ten either. That show grossed only $635,545 out of a potential $994,201, selling 72% of capacity that week.

And the infamous 2001 Tony Award Winner "Best Musical" *The Producers*—which won the most Tony Awards in Broadway history—was also not in the Top Ten . . . even though that show grossed $979,561 out of a potential $1,042,163, and sold at 83% capacity last week.

It was *Mamma Mia!*—a show which won *no* Tony Awards at

all—that is not only still in the Top Ten (as it has been since opening in October 2001), but is firmly holding on to that No. 1 slot . . . selling at 101.1% of capacity.

Overall total receipts for the week ending December 14, 2003 was $16,838,471. And even though attendance that week dipped by 1.8% from the previous weeks totals, it was not so shabby a showing in the days and weeks leading up to the notoriously slow holiday weeks.

So what does all this tell us?

It tells us that Broadway has changed. The *business* of Broadway has changed. The content of what's being produced has changed. And the manner in which audiences purchase tickets has changed.

So yes, we've been hearing for years and years that Broadway's dying. Many, have eagerly proclaimed it's already dead. But guess what? It's still here. And it's doing better than ever. Financially, at least. It's just . . . evolved. That's all. But its still going strong nonetheless.

As Alex Cohen told his theatre managements students a few years back, don't expect to find Sam Shepherd on Broadway these days. Unless, of course, Brad Pitt or Ben Stiller is cast in the lead.

Don't expect to see very many original musicals on Broadway these days either. Look more to what those potential musicals have evolved into—the spectacle; the Broadway version of the Las Vegas spectacular. It's glitz, and it's entertaining, and it looks amazing . . . and most of all, audiences will feel good when they leave the theatre. They might or might not be humming a memorable new tune for very long, but they'll have a great time nonetheless.

And don't expect to see many new American plays on Broadway these days either. That just won't happen. Unless, of course, the play has tried out in various regional theatres around the country, and succeeded to unbelievable levels of the imagination. Unless, of course, Mr. Pitt or Mr. Stiller wishes to take a perhaps career-killing risk. New American drama just doesn't seem to sell anymore on Broadway. And that's a very sad statement to make.

Clearly, we see the Broadway theatre is in transition. Moving us into a new and yet unknown spectrum of entertainment styles and content.

But to understand the full story, we'll need to take a look at the other side of the pond . . . to London's West End.

A Candid Look at London's West End

January 2004

EVA
Don't cry for me Argentina
For I am ordinary, unimportant
And undeserving of such attention
Unless we all are—I think we all are
So share my glory, so share my coffin
So share my glory, so share my coffin

CHE
It's our funeral too

—Tim Rice
Evita: Andrew Lloyd Webber and Tim Rice

Part Two—

All the World's a Stage

I doubt anyone would argue that during the 1970s and 1980s, the West End greatly contributed to giving an international focus to London as a—if not *the*—center of big popular musical entertainment. I'm referring of course to the production of such musicals as *Jesus Christ Superstar, Cats, Evita, Phantom, Les Miserables, Starlight Express*, and perhaps *Miss Saigon* as well. And along with that great success, many restaurants, shops, and other ancillary businesses followed suit, making London—and perhaps, more importantly London's West End—*the* place to go.

There were several people responsible for driving that transformation: of course Cameron Mackintosh, Andrew Lloyd Webber and Tim Rice, and perhaps Bill Kenwright as well. They had the foresight. They had the vision. And most of all, they were willing to take the risks.

London is, after all, a theatre town. It has always been, and perhaps it will always be. There are currently forty-eight legitimate theatres in London's West End. And at the time of this writing, all of them are lit—as they have been for quite some time. That is, of course, in sharp contrast to Broadway—which has thirty-four legitimate theatres in its theatre district, with only thirty of those currently lit.

Why had London become such a leader in theatrical production?

First off, we must consider the practicalities. Production costs are quite a bit lower in London than they are on Broadway. And it stands to reason then—if the show costs less to produce, the producer has less to recoup before profit, and so ticket prices might be less as well. And indeed they are. Theatre tickets to most West End performances are still currently lower than they are on Broadway—but as you can see, not really by very much.

	London	New York
Disney's *The Lion King*	[1] £55.90 / $98.64	$110.00
Chicago	£52.60 / $92.81	$100.00
The Phantom of the Opera	£54.20 / $95.64	$100.00

---

[1] Currency Exchange rate as of 2003.12.22 20:43:30 GMT.
   50.00 GBP United Kingdom Pounds = **88.2518 USD** United States Dollars
   1 GBP = 1.76504 USD 1 USD = 0.566561 GBP

It should be noted, however, that some of the newer shows—some of the more successful shows currently running in London's West End—are just beginning to surpass New York ticket prices:

	London	New York
Mamma Mia!	£63.45 / $111.97	$100.00
Jerry Springer—The Musical	£65.80 / $116.11	Not Yet Open

So even with the production cost savings, it seems West End producers are beginning to realize that charging higher prices for theatre tickets is something the market will continue to bear. London theatre ticket bargains? Perhaps soon, a thing of the past.

In comparison to New York, London seems to have a much more solid and enthusiastic theatre culture. New York is more of a movie-going town; London is not. Television is far more popular in the United States than it is int the United Kingdom.

When someone is in London for the day with some hours to spare, they just might run off to buy a last-minute theatre ticket . . . something that just doesn't happen in New York City very much any more.

But what makes the West End so different from Broadway is that even though some of the top ticket prices in the West End are beginning to edge up to Broadway levels, and at times even surpass them, West End producers offer far more tickets at affordable rates; and the lowest ticket prices available for purchase are also quite a bit lower than their counterparts in New York currently offer.

	Lowest Ticket Price in London	Lowest Ticket Price in New York
Chicago	£19.65 / $34.68	$67.50
Disney's *The Lion King*	£26.35 / $46.50	$68.00
The Phantom of the Opera	£25.50 / $45.00	$55.00
Mamma Mia!	£29.65 / $52.33	$61.25
Jerry Springer—The Musical	£32.95 / $ 58.15	Due to Open 2004/2005

And making biggest news this season was, of course, Nicholas Hytner's Travelex £10 Season at the National Theatre, in which tickets to the NT's South Bank's largest auditorium were offered for less than a first-run movie ticket at some London cinemas.

Who Am I anyway?

In a way, the British have always felt that the theatre was theirs. And even with groundbreaking productions like a Tennessee Williams play or musicals like *West Side Story* and *Oklahoma*—for us in America, we never have. I believe we in America are far more passive theatre-goers, than active.

In some ways, American audiences are waiting to be told what to see. They seem to leave the decision of which shows to see to the critics. Whereas in England, it seems critics are writing for someone far more willing to throw down the review and say "I don't care what the reviewer says; that sounds like an interesting play. I want to see it."

Nonetheless, with all the great theatre-going spirit one finds in the United Kingdom these days, the state of the theatrical community in London's West End is currently a bit unsettled.

In 2002 Andrew Lloyd Weber and Cameron Mackintosh

held a rather unusual joint press conference; unusual in the sense that one rarely sees these two theatrical giants together in the same room, let alone on the same dais.

Sir Cameron spoke about the concern many West End producers have regarding the future of the industry. He mentioned how audience figures were down 10-15% from previous year's totals. Yet he felt that the dip in business was caused by the physical condition of the West End itself . . . not the shows.

Crime and Grime were to blame. It was the crime, he believed, that was keeping audiences away; especially the crime on Shaftesbury Avenue—one of the West End's main thoroughfares. He berated London's rapidly deteriorating transport system. And he lamented too about the impossible parking situation in most areas surrounding the West End. It was not an environment which welcomed theatre-goers, at any stage.

Mackintosh likened it to living in a house for ten or fifteen years—enjoying it so much that you fail to notice that it's getting shabby, and in desperate need of repair.

Andrew Lloyd Webber compared the current situation in London with that of New York City in the 1970's. New York, he said, might have been in the same or perhaps in a far worse state in those years, but the New York City government—in association with the theatrical community and a number of the city's leading citizens—addressed the problem rather smartly.

They first initiated an aggressive plan to clean up Times Square—a multi-year project arguably driven by the Disney organization's purchase of the deteriorating New Amsterdam Theater and it's ambitious refurbishment plan. In addition, massive subway renovations and increased safety patrols encouraged both New Yorkers as well as tourists to visit the theatre district and to feel far more comfortable there. At the same time, other new and more family-driven businesses began to see the inevitable future of a renewed Times Square, and so they too flocked to the area giving it a kinder, safer, "look and feel." As did the most recent mayoral "quality of life" campaign, which relocated the more adult-type businesses—which, for so long had dominated the Times Square arena—to other differently-zoned parts of Manhattan.

And with it all came the highly successful *I Love NY* marketing campaign which helped give the entire concept a very popular spin.

To address Messrs. Lloyd Webber and Mackintosh's concerns, it is wonderful to note that the London Police force has already launched *Operation Victory* whose objective it is to improve the quality of life in the West End utilizing many of the tactics proven so successful on the other side of the pond. And we certainly wish them the well with their efforts; it's not an easy task.

So indeed—after years of the West End *leading* the theatrical world, they might now be eager to establish their own version of the current Broadway model.

In a way, it's as if the West End is seeking a new identity—passively or pro-actively trying to find a creative antidote to their very own identity crisis. And when one looks a bit deeper, it appears it's not just a physical rehab they're after, but a conceptual and strategic rehab as well.

One Hand Washing The Other

When one looks at the theatrical mix these days—what's playing in London's West End—one of the first thing one sees is that the West End is getting *branded*.

Many commercial theatres are beginning to tether themselves to a specific theatre or not-for-profit production company. And in this sense, they are becoming a bit more pro-active in creating their futures. It's a strategy which has really taken off since the

Old Vic first signed an agreement with Matthew Bourne's former "Adventures in Motion Pictures" company several years ago.

Some theatres have restructured completely and hired in-house producers, more or less guaranteeing programming over a season—and here, the Old Vic was once again at the forefront. In 2003 they hired the popular American Academy Award-winning actor Kevin Spacey to be the director of their new Production Company.

Other London theatres have also jumped on the proverbial bandwagon. And many of them are aligning with Off-West End production companies, such as the Albery Theatre. Or even with an out-of-town theatrical troupe, such as the Whitehall Theatre has done with fringe producer Dominic Dromgoole.

By pursuing this strategy—by creating a partnership of sorts . . . an "identity" . . . via these alliances—many London theatres now feel they can better target and therefore better expand their specific audience base.

The hoped-for result, of course, is a synergy between the subsidized and the commercial spheres of the industry—with the former helping to insure that the latter doesn't simply give itself over exclusively to big brassy musical productions.

To be, or not to be . . .

And so I'd like to pose a question which has been no doubt asked for ages: Should the theatre be about creating art, educating, provoking thought . . . or should it just be about entertainment and making money?

Indeed, art, educating, provoking thought have always been key mainstays in theatre for centuries. And that's all well and good. But the theatre is a business after all. And without brisk commerce, theatre will die. So finding the commercial possibilities in serious dramatic theatre today is a great challenge.

Many people in the West End community believe that the recently refurbished Royal Court Theatre can take a great deal of credit for what commercial appetite now exists for dramas and plays. And we do, in fact, see more and more dramatic works being produced all throughout London and its environs. It's apparent that many theatre managements throughout the West End are getting wise to the fact that even though the big splashy musicals clearly have the focus and perhaps bring in the largest revenues—that creating an appetite for drama, they believe, is really the wave of the future.

Yes, it's about creating the art. And it's also about creating the marketplace in which that art will survive. It's got to be about theatre owners and production companies taking ownership . . . taking control . . . and trying to influence the work that is going into their theatres. Trying to create a market for what is being written today and for where theatre—as an institution—is going.

Producers and theatrical companies have got to be more and more interested in not just the "one-offs" but in actually developing a strategy from which they will know what their theatre will be doing in a year's time so that profitable programming can be confirmed quite far in advance. This is essential today in a marketplace driven by marketing and advertising; by strategic and group sales; and by key merchandising/sponsorship opportunities as well.

And so . . . is this newer concept of creating alliances and driving the marketplace shaking up the mainstream? You bet it is. And it's a good thing too. We're all better off for it. For as long as theatres are full of good product, what ever is the difference?

Often times, a little shake-up is good.

And finding more and more ways to strengthen the *business* of theatre is a very good thing. Every producer I know would agree that the theatre venture in itself is inherently fragile . . . and so there's a real advantage in being able to book a theatre for a particular stretch of time, knowing there's going to be a consistency of good work produced within that space. And what, I believe, has been missing up until now is the commercial mix that "branding" a theatre might allow.

A healthy theatre community—a healthy West End—is one where you have an *Art* or a *Stones In His Pockets*, and *The Phantom of the Opera* and a *Bombay Dreams,* all running alongside one another—in addition to the subsidized/not-for-profit productions. It's about balance . . . and not unlike it is in the stock market, it's about diversification. And so far, it seems, London has been able to handle that balance and diversification far greater than that city's counterpart in the Americas.

But such alliances need not be only domestic; international partners can indeed be profitable as well. And in this light, it's interesting to note that The Royal National Theatre announced it has recently signed a $1.35 million deal with two American producers giving them the first right to transfer any of the National's shows to the United States. As Jason Zinoman wrote in *The New York Times* "The deal between the National Theater, one of the premier cultural institutions in the world, and two producers—Bob Boyett and Ostar Productions, run by Bill Haber—reflects the increasing popularity of partnerships between commercial producers and subsidized theater companies, the unflagging interest among American theater producers in all things British, and a new direction for the National, which recently changed leadership." All of this, or course, is the brainchild of Nicholas Hytner, the National Theatre's new Artistic Director.

"We thought it was a good idea that when we had a show for American audiences that we had a quick, direct and well-trodden path" Hynter said. "We liked Bob and Bill because, to be blunt, we couldn't find anyone on Broadway with a bad word to say about them."

For those skeptics concerned that such an alliance would bring a more commercial taint to the National's programming, Nicholas Hytner was emphatic.

"We are a National Theatre of Britain" he said "and it is our job to reflect our nation. It's Bill and Bob's job to use their intuition to choose which of these shows will be of interest in America."

Life Upon The Wicked Stage

So with London's crime and grime problems well on their way to eradication, and the theatre community's new concept of "theatrical branding" well settling in, and with the great balance of commercial to non-for-profit productions more and more taking hold, one would readily think that London's West End is well on it's way to solidifying a keen new identity and perhaps once again being on the verge of leading the world in innovative theatrical content.

But after taking a closer look at the last few London seasons, one can easily see why such is not the case. And why many a West End critic have sarcastically called those seasons "Made in the USA."

There actually has been an influx of American shows to the West End these last few seasons, several of them in their original productions. Some think of it as a long-overdue attempt to re-dress what many have called the great theatrical imbalance of a few year's back, because—as we all know—the theatrical transatlantic traffic for the past twenty years or so has generally gone the other way.

On Broadway, some kind of theatrical history was made in 2002 when eight English or Irish stagings—including those of several American plays such as Eugene O'Neill's *The Iceman Cometh*—all opened within ten weeks of each other. In some theatrical circles, New York was dubbed "London on the Hudson."

Yet surprisingly—perhaps somewhat stealthily—the last two London theatre seasons have been awash in American exports.

Many locals do lament the Americanization of the London stage, with its adaptations of Hollywood movies and reliance on brand name celebrities—whether its the "let it go" spirit of *The Full Monty*—easily London's biggest musical opening since *The Lion King*—or some other theatrical transfers from New York like *Chicago, Fosse, Kiss Me Kate, Side Man, Bash, Wit* . . . all with their American creative teams intact.

Those of a certain age might recall when American plays and musicals in London meant something special. When American productions helped to set the standard. When musicals like *West Side Story* and *Oklahoma* and *The Sound Of Music* actually had longer runs in the West End than they did on Broadway. Yes . . . the good old days!

But suddenly then, with great fanfare, the era of the megamusical hit both Atlantic shores, and the transfer of American plays and musicals was slowed considerably. The business, it seemed, was overrun with epic stagings written and directed and produced by only a chosen few. And through it all, little else was able to rear its head, let alone thrive.

Richard Eyre, the former artistic director of the Royal National Theater recently said that he fell in love with the American theatre even before he fell in love with theatre as a whole. The British stuff, he said, seemed incredibly bloodless. But with O'Neill and Williams . . . drama suddenly had fangs.

How ironic then that many of the London critic now-a-days regard so much American drama as toothless, and readily bare their *own* fangs to dismember many a New York hit.

More than one West End producer has remarked that London critics seem to be horrified by the phrase "Broadway hit." They apparently prefer to nurture homegrown stars like David Hare or Tom Stoppard (as they should)—or even *discover* American playwrights—rather than follow a parade of writers that originated elsewhere, or have succeeded elsewhere. Ironically, it could be said that anonymity in the United States might represent an American writer's best chance for success in London.

But setting aside what some of the London critics might be saying, it's still quite difficult for American playwrights of any stature to get produced in the West End.

Playwright David Hare said recently "It really isn't easy for American writers in London. There are three or four name American writers who are on the modern syllabus whose plays will always pack theatres, and will be given a hearing. But we are extremely intolerant for the row immediately below that."

Lucy Davies, then literary manager of the Donmar Warehouse and producer of their "American Series" called some of these new American plays by fairly unknown American authors "such an enormously un-mined area. There's a real one-way traffic of our finest British plays, particularly to New York . . . and I've noticed a lot of anger among young American writers. The chances are that a young British playwright is going to get a play on Broadway before homegrown talent. We're sending all our plays over there, but we don't seem to be importing anything back. And that's a tragedy."

And apparently, the controversy continues. And it's a fun thing to watch. So let's take a close look to see just how out of balance the transatlantic theatrical trade really is.

If you can make it there . . .

Some of the American plays and playwrights who have opened in London in recent seasons are:

- Tony Kushner's *Homebody/Kabul* (Young Vic)
- Adly Guirgus's *Jesus Hopped the "A" Train* (Donmar Warehouse)
- Kenneth Lonergan's *Lobby Hero* (Donmar Warehouse)
- David Auburn's *Proof* (Donmar Warehouse)
- Richard Greenberg's *Take Me Out* (Donmar Warehouse)

Along with the world premiers of two "new" young American playwrights:

- Kia Corthron's *Breath, Boom* (Royal Court)
- Christopher Shinn's *Other People*

Many of these authors and playwrights have had difficulty getting produced in the United States where the risk-taking landscape is far greater, and so they were subsequently snatched up by interested West End producers. What is important to note here is that when new American plays premiere in London, there really appears to be great interest—audiences are fascinated; the business is brisk—so naturally I predict this trend will continue well on into the future.

When discussing the New York/London theatrical trade, the conversation inevitably leads to the *vast cultural differences* in what audiences will accept in the United States and what they will accept in the United Kingdom. Most believe the two audience groups are quite different in their likes and dislikes. And many producers find it quite difficult to predict just what will succeed in either city.

The typically American porch drama doesn't do well in London these days; I doubt it would do well in the United States either.

The hit American musicals *Rent* and *Hedwig and the Angry Inch* didn't take off in London at all. Similarly—Hamish McColl and Sean Foley's *The Play What I Wrote* struggled for weeks in New York before finally succumbing to a difficult box office downturn.

It seems the West End looks for a more fast-flowing, abstract, experimental drama; that's what appears to be what has been emerging in the United Kingdom these last few seasons. Although I personally would have thought that John Cameron Mitchell and Stephen Trask's *Hedwig and the Angry Inch* was just that kind of piece.

Commenting on why some American plays often do *not* do well in Britain, the successful English director Matthew Warchus (*Art; Follies*) said "I don't think it has totally to do with nationality. It's to do with the level of enthusiasm generated in the theatre. And I don't think London has nearly as vibrant and enthusiastic a theatre culture as New York."

Actually, Mr. Warchus' comment surprised me. Most people in the industry feel just the opposite. I believe it's really about how open the theatrical community is for new and different works. New and different voices. And London, to me, seems far more willing to entertain new and meaningful conceptual ideas.

This is a town after all which had *three* Ibsen plays running simultaneously in the West End in 2003; something you'd never see on Broadway.

It's becoming more and more clear, however, that when American plays and musicals do make their way to London, they should at least begin with their original productions—that is, with their original casts and creative teams intact—not unlike most London-to-New York transfers. (*The Shape of Things*, for example)

Recently, I visited a friend who is currently the House Manager of one of London's leading theatres. We were discussing this transatlantic transfer of shows, and I asked if he had yet seen the revival of *Chicago*, currently playing at London's Adelphi Theatre.

My friend looked at me as though I were mad. "Of course not" he said to me. "Why would I want to see that?"

I told him that *Chicago* was really a very good show—a great production, in fact. It's Bob Fosse, after all. What could be better than that?"

"But that's just the point. That's a show that is driven by dance. In England" he said to me "we just don't have the dancers you have in the States. They lack the experience and the sophistication. Most of all, they lack the style. Why would I want to see an American show that's essentially all about dance and American dance style, with British dancers? I'd rather come see it in New York. I'd rather see the real thing."

Now on the other side of the pond, the American appetite for English work appears only to intensify over time . . . we just can't get enough of it. So it can be quite dismaying when the traffic is reversed to find that the enthusiasm is not.

So I did some research about this New York-London rivalry . . . and this is what I discovered.

What Are Some of the Critics Saying?

John Peter in *The Sunday Times of London* is quoted as saying: "you can take a show out of New York, but you cannot take New York out of the show." This he wrote of the West End production of the American musical *Rent*, before deriding the late Jonathan Larson's "well-meaning but oppressive political correctness that sometimes makes you recoil in despair."

Mr. Peter's review was actually one of the gentler ones; three of his colleagues went so far as to imply, however facetiously, that Mr. Larson's death on the eve of the New York opening, was a canny career move.

Conversely, the musical *Chicago* . . . currently in the West End . . . received glowing notices in London. But if you think about it—that is a show that portrays Americans as hard-edged and cynical—everything the singularly openhearted *Rent*, for all its real flaws, does not.

Famed critic Nick Curtis wrote in *The Evening Standard* of Eve Ensler's *The Vagina Monologues* . . . "the tone is an uneasy mixture of the wry and the wrenching, of sit-down comedy and theatre as therapy . . . and oh . . . it's from New York in case you hadn't guessed."

Edward Albee's *The Play About The Baby*, which had a successful Off-Broadway run in 2002, was received in London by uniformly hostile critics, while those from American critics were only positive.

It seems the more prizes a show has won in the United States (Jonathan Larson's *Rent* won both the Pulitzer Prize and the Tony Award for Best Musical), the more that seems to irk some British critics.

The Full Monty which won NO Tony Awards in 2002, opened in the West End to raves.

By contrast—in New York—success seems to become success. Everyone is dying to see the latest hit from London. And that's what's so wonderful about working in the New York theatrical community—its openness; its desire for new and exciting work, no matter where it comes from.

But there is a bit of a hit-flop mentality on Broadway was well—if it's a hit, I'll see it; if it's not a hit, I'm not interested. And that's also what's dangerous; that's what's making producers in New York take less and less risk.

On top of all this, it seems the once "golden age" of the big costly musicals appears to be winding down. And as well all know, most of those splashy epic musicals from past seasons were first produced in London's West End.

Cameron Mackintosh's *Martin Guarre* didn't make it to Broadway; his infamous revival of *Oklahoma* opened in New York in 2002 to lukewarm reviews and closed within the year; *Cats* has closed in New York after eighteen years, and in London after twenty years. So has *Starlight Express*, and *Miss Saigon* . . .

Andrew Lloyd Webber's *The Beautiful Game* had a tremendous struggle in the West End (even with fairly good reviews) and has no plans of a Broadway opening. His *Whistle Down the Wind* couldn't even make it past pre-Broadway tryouts at Washington's Kennedy Center.

Even one of Cameron Mackintosh's latest successes—*The Witches of Eastwick*—had struggled, then scaled itself down before moving to a much smaller theatre. It finally closed resulting in total loss of investment.

Hey, Mr. Producer!

Cameron Mackintosh is perhaps the only "giant" we have left in the business. He's truly a rare and unique impresario still willing to take risks—although some might argue that with his great wealth and his great success over the years, he's perhaps the only producer who *could* still take risks in this new marketplace.

Mackintosh is a hands-on producer who works closely with his creative team . . . asking questions . . . making suggestions . . . driving creative . . . he's ever present during the entire process. And indeed that's a rarity in an industry driven by producers who are simply in it for the business opportunity.

As we learned from Part One of *Bright Lights, Big Changes* most shows on Broadway are produced by committee. Needless to say, this is an extremely dangerous practice for the future of innovative creative ideas, as it tends to take everything down to the lowest common denominator. So it's marvelous to see someone like Cameron Mackintosh still interested, and still working . . . still taking a strong hand . . . and thank God for it.

And let's face it. There's something to be said about a Cameron Mackintosh production, whether you like the particular story or not. One has to admit his shows are exceedingly well produced. Clearly, they bear his imprint. Indeed, Sir Mackintosh has created a *brand* of his own. And the value of that is tremendous.

But when you look at his most recent body of work, it's clear that even Cameron Mackintosh now seems to be producing only "safe" projects these days—revivals of classic musicals. *Oliver*, *Oklahoma*, *My Fair Lady*. And, of course, his newest production—a joint venture with Disney Theatricals which will bring the ever-popular *Mary Poppins* to the London stage in 2004 (film-to-stage transfer).

Cameron Mackintosh recently told me that he's not really

interested in producing any new (original) shows just now. "The theatre is too much in transition" he said to me one sunny afternoon while seated in his impressive Bedford Square offices. "It's static; treading water, so to speak. I'm only interested in keeping my current shows open as long as I can." [Mackintosh was of course referring to *The Phantom of the Opera* currently celebrating it's 16th year on Broadway; both *The Phantom of the Opera* and *Les Miserables* are still running strong in the West End, and touring world-wide as well]

"And revivals" I added.

He smiled broadly. "*Oliver* was the very first show I produced that was a success, so it was fitting to bring it back a few years ago. And *Oklahoma* and *My Fair Lady*? Those are simply two magnificent musicals which I've admired for a very long time. So why not?"

So if indeed the "golden age" of the mega-epic-musicals is waning, just what are some of the newer trends in theatrical production in London's West End?

The biggest trend is one you've already read about. One, I'm afraid, that is rampant on both sides of the Atlantic. And that is the current trend toward creating theatre as an event. Making it bigger than life. Now, that's not such a bad thing in itself. But some say producers are trying just a bit too hard to make their show more than what it is. They don't trust the content. They are more apt to give you the sizzle, and forget about the steak.

And if you're not going to make theatre an event in the mega-epic-musical way—through lavish special effects and environmental design—the only way then is through star power.

In recent months, there has been a strategic interest in adding "stars" to the mix on the London stage. And just as this trend has evolved on Broadway, these may or may not necessarily be the "stars" one would normally associate with the London stage. Or in fact would *want* to associate with the London stage. So again, we might want to use the term "celebrities" rather than stars.

Not too long ago, The Royal Shakespeare Company announced that it would dismantle its permanent company of actors and abandon its London base at the Barbican Hall in order to attract bigger stars and present more productions in the "showier" West End. The RSC producers clearly felt that this is the only way to go today, in order to guarantee good box office. It creates great media hype, and therefore great PR and solid word-of-mouth.

Here are just some examples of how London producers are beginning to add star/celebrities into the mix: Jerry Hall in *The Graduate*; MacCauley Culkin in Richard Nelson's *Madame Melville;* Nicole Kidman in *The Blue Room;* Brandon Frazier in *Cat on a Hot Tin Roof;* and of course Madonna in *Up For Grabs.* And the most recent announcement that pop diva Mariah Carey will appear in a revival of Terence Rattigan's 1956 *The Sleeping Prince* in 2004 only proves this point. *The Sleeping Prince* is perhaps best known for being the source of the Marilyn Monroe/Laurence Olivier movie *The Prince and Showgirl.*

Clearly, none of these names would ordinarily come to mind when thinking of great stage moments in theatrical history. But today, that's immaterial. It's what sells that counts. Whether the star/celebrity is talented or not is simply irrelevant.

Let's be frank. Does anyone really believe that *Up For Grabs* would ever have been produced if Madonna's name was not attached to it?

Unlike New York, London still hosts numerous *true* stage stars—Maggie Smith, Judy Dench, Joan Plowright, Jonathan Price . . . just to name a few. Yet it's becoming increasingly rare these days to see these great actors standing behind the footlights.

There are, however, quite a few younger stage actors following closely in the queue. London seems to have far more solid and reputable stage actors than New York—those specifically trained for the stage. If you need to understand why, there might be a very simple explanation.

I believe the desire to be a successful stage actor in the United Kingdom is still an admired tradition. It's a learned craft, and the training, I'm afraid, is far more serious and disciplined in the UK than it is in the United States, where today many young people simply want to be on stage or on TV or in the film industry solely to become famous and reap the financial rewards. The United Kingdom still boasts young acting students who want to be an actor simply to be a fine actor—nothing more. And these are very different motives indeed.

Also, London is a city which headquarters both the theatre and the film industries combined. So the actors and stronger—more versatile; far more able to swing between the two media quickly and easily.

In the United Stages, we have the theatre and TV/film industries separated by a very distant three thousand miles—from coast to coast. Most actors then focus their training on one discipline or the other—rarely both. And so the acting skill in the United States then is far more limited.

Nonetheless, producers often cast their shows simply to be clever or unusual and sometimes—even with such novelty casting—they do indeed get it right and responsibly maintain the integrity of the author's word: Jessica Lang in *Long Days Journey Into Night;* Calista Flockhart in *The Philadelphia Story*, are just two examples. Notice here—both solid actresses, but both American.

As in New York, this trend is here and it's here to stay. It's certainly changing the landscape, and we can only see where that leads.

Indeed, as we settle in to a new century, there seems to be change all around us. And why should the theatre—West End Theatre, specifically—be immune to that change?

There have been a number of administrative changes within London's theatrical companies recently. And it will be interesting to see just how much their operations will be effected because of those changes, if at all.

In April 2003 Trevor Nunn turned over the artistic control of the National Theatre to Nicholas Hytner. And I'm pleased to say that at the time of this writing—as Mr. Hytner's first season at the NT comes to a close—the reviews have been grand. There was no denying the excitement emanating from David Leveaux's production of Tom Stoppard's *Jumpers*, and from Howard Davies' production of the Eugene O'Neill epic *Mourning Becomes Electra*. And then there was Michael Blakemore's amazing staging of Michael Frayn's *Democracy*.

Think about it—in contrast to such notable productions at the National this season—what hope did the commercial West End have? Not a lot, amid a climate of failed star-vehicles such as Patrick Stewart's *The Master Builder*, and the latest in the seemingly endless line of back-catalog rock musicals . . . *Tonight's the Night*—the Rod Stewart Musical.

Both Adrian Noble and Director Edward Hall have left the Royal Shakespeare Company—artistic director Adrian Noble was under attack for spending too much time on "outside commercial projects" (*Chitty Chitty Bang Bang*, among others). Michael Boyd, Noble's former Associate Director was named as replacement in July 2002.

Michael Attenborough has taken over as the new Artistic Director of the Almeida.

And of course Sam Mendes has turned over the artistic control of the Donmar Warehouse to Michael Grandage—Mr. Grandage was the Associate Director of Donmar since 2000.

The West End Goes to the Movies

And not unlike on Broadway, the West End has not escaped the movie trend. The last few seasons have brought numerous transfers from screen-to-stage—*Sunset Boulevard*, *Saturday Night Fever*, *Peggy Sue Got Married*, *Whistle Down the Wind*, and *The Graduate*.

In 2003, it was announced that Director Matthew Warchus and designer Rob Howell will soon be staging a musical version of the J.R. Tolkien literary classic *The Lord of the Rings*—no doubt tapping into the great success of the recent film trilogy.

A musical based on the cult classic *Barbarella* was just announced. Billed as the "sexy space musical", the score will be written by the *Eurythmic*'s Dave Steward. Although this production will originate in Vienna and not in London's West End, it clearly shows the eagerness producers have to jump onto the film-to-stage bandwagon and find new product. It's a clear sign too of their not being enough new product to produce.

And as this book goes to print, the Theatre Royal Haymarket announced that a stage version of the successful movie *When Harry Met Sally* will open in February 2004 starring Alyson Hannigan—co-star of the American television series *Buffy The Vampire Slayer*—and Luke Perry. The show will be directed by Loveday Ingram. Again—an American film; by an American writer (Nora Ephron), starring two American TV celebrities. No doubt the London critics will have a field day.

Tickets! Tickets!

When in London, I like to purchase my tickets direct from the box office. I have always received the finest service there, and I've been able to obtain some amazing seat locations, often times at last minute.

Not unlike the famous TKTS Ticket Booth on Times Square, London also offers numerous opportunities to purchase discounted or half-price theatre tickets. The best, perhaps, is the large Ticket Office located on the south side of Leicester Square in the clock tower building. The office is open Mon-Sat 10am – 7pm. Sun 12 noon – 3pm. Tickets are sold at half price, plus a modest service charge of £2.50.

In addition, there are other discounted ticket offices located throughout Covent Garden. These are really ticket brokers who *might* offer discounts. And some of them have been known to issue counterfeit tickets which the theatres will not honor. So you might be best served by using the main Ticket Office in Leicester Square.

"The most important thing in life is honesty.
If you can fake that, you've just about got it made."
—Groucho Marx

Part Three—
At The End Of The Day

So it's here we find ourselves—mid-decade, at the beginning of a new century; a new millennium. An amazing concept in itself.

The theatre—on both sides of the Atlantic—continues to evolve. And many forces are responsible for that evolution: societal growth and desires, economic realities, and most of all—the need and the desire to have something new to say.

Theatre, after all, is the art of the spoken word. It cannot exist without a voice—a point of view. It cannot grow without writers willing to dedicate their craft passionately to the stage. We're losing those writers faster than I can type. We're in a theatrical pandemic, and we don't even know it. Let there be no doubt—the theatre as we once knew it *is* dying. It's the *art* of the theatre that's dying. And in its place, we find entertainment for the masses.

> *"We [producers] are spinning out of control in pursuit of*
> *'What do people want?' I've been around long enough to*
> *remember a time when we weren't worried about what*
> *people wanted. We did what we wanted, and people came*
> *along.*
>
> —Harold Prince
>
> SOURCE: *The New York Times*—September 9, 2003

If producers are clever enough to mask middle-of-the-road content; if producers continue to be willing to sell any idea for a buck; if we only produce producers who are able to make an audience believe they're actually going to "the theatre" when in reality they're going to a marvelously man-made simulation of what was once the great theatrical experience—then, and only then, will the industry succeed in its dangerous path toward mediocrity.

The Music of the Night

At one time, Broadway scores drove pop music and culture— *Standing On the Corner* (*Fiorello!*); *What Kind of Fool Am I?* (Anthony Newley's *Stop the World, I Want To Get Off*); *The Impossible Dream* (*Man of La Mancha*); *Send In The Clowns* (Stephen Sondheim's *A Little Night Music*). Even the more "contemporary" musicals such as *Jesus Christ Superstar* and *Hair* gave us several popular hits—*I Don't Know How To Love Him* and *Let The Sun Shine In* respectively.

Today however, it seems as if we're living in a time where the opposite is actually true. Where the content of our stage shows— and perhaps our culture overall—is what's affected by the popular music around us.

Of the eleven currently-running musical "non-revivals" that have opened on Broadway since the autumn of 2000, just six have had original scores. The rest—simply a recycling of old music, pop music, and/or compendiums of a host of other peoples' music (*Contact*).

It's ironic, in a way. As there is no shortage of exciting musical talent in New York City and around the country: Michael John LaChiusa, Andrew Lippa, Adam Guettel, Jason Robert Brown, David Yazbek, Jeanine Tesori, and many many others. Yet they rarely get produced.

Why? Many producers feel it's simply too big a risk to try to sell a new young composer to their audiences. Yet ironically, even some composers who have greatly succeeded in years past have been having difficulty getting produced on Broadway. Stephen Sondheim's most recent musical *Bounce*, and John Kander and Fred Ebb's latest musical *The Visit*, have both been abandoned prior to their 2003 New York debuts due to mediocre reviews while on the road.

Producers today seem to believe the public is only willing to accept stories and concepts and music they already know. Is that really true? Or is it just speculation on the part of some very skittish Broadway and West End producers?

As Bruce Webber states so eloquently in a recent *The New York Times* article—"it's enough to make you scratch your head and ask: whither Broadway music?"

The Digital Revolution

The Internet has become a major factor in the production of Broadway shows—in particular, Internet Chat Rooms.

In year's past, taking a show "out of town" to Boston or Philadelphia or Hartford prior to that show's New York City opening would be an important step in its development. It gave the creative and technical teams ample time to "work out the kinks" far away from the glaring eyes of Broadway and its critics.

But those days are gone. And Internet chatter in the various Broadway and West End chat rooms [e.g. *All That Chat* (talkinbroadway.com/forum); BroadwayWorld.com] is now so constant and ever-ready, that any negative word-of-mouth that at one time a producer might have been able to suppress, will today spread like wild-fire. And it can ultimately be disastrous.

Many of the participants in these online chat rooms are quite competitive in trying to be the very first to see (and therefore review) a new musical or play. It is well known that one online personality actually left The Eugene O'Neill Theatre and ran down West 49th Street to an Internet café during the intermission of the very first preview of the Broadway musical *The Full Monty* in order to post a review; and returned to the theatre just in time for the second act to begin (which he also reviewed shortly thereafter).

It is still unclear as to the actual impact these website chat rooms (and their personalities) have on the success or failure of a show. Although it is often said that early negative Internet buzz regarding the 2000 Boston tryout of the musical *Seussical* just might have killed that show's chances of a successful Broadway run even before the show ever opened its doors at New York's Richard Rodgers Theatre.

The Internet too has changed the way we do business. E-commerce sites are ubiquitous, and have revolutionized the way consumers purchase tickets. With the flick of a key, you can be off to see the hit of the season. It's easy, it's fast, and you never even have to see or deal with another human being. What more could anyone want?

What A Remarkable Age This Is!

When one looks back at the last few decades of theatrical production on both sides of the Atlantic, an apparent pattern can be seen in the style of the shows themselves, and in the ways in which they were produced.

The 50s could be considered the decade of the romantic storyline (*South Pacific, Can Can, West Side Story, Carnival*; the 60s—the decade of change and great cultural revolution (*Hair, Don't Bother Me, I Can't Cope*). It was simply about the message.

The 70s brought us the decade of the dancer—Bob Fosse and Michael Bennett led the way, the first to give dancers a voice and a character to portray (*Pippin, Chicago, A Chorus Line, Dancin'*). These show's were daring and honest—often-times quite personal in bringing forth their raw human revelations.

In the 1980s, we saw the epic mega-musical consume Broadway and the West End, if not the world. At times, it was storytelling at its finest; other times, just glitz. Nonetheless, it was this apparent renaissance of Broadway and the West End which led to it becoming a billion dollar industry worldwide. (*The Phantom of the Opera, Les Miserables, Miss Saigon, Aspects of Love, Chess, Cats, Starlight Express, Time*).

Finally, the 90s brought us not much of anything. One or two producers reaped the enormous profits of their mega successes of the 80s. And little if any new or creative work was notable at all.

And today—it seems it's pop music alone that drives Broadway and the West End. Billy Joel (*Movin' Out*), Abba (*Mamma Mia!*), Boy George (*Taboo*), Peter Allen (*The Boy From Oz*), Queen (*We Will Rock You*), Rod Stewart (*Tonight's The Night*), and a host of others. It's a Broadway/West End jukebox of sorts. It's where we are creatively, and it's no doubt where we will stay for the near future at least.

In the aftermath of September 11th it appears audiences do not really want to be challenged; do not really want to think. They want nothing to tweak their emotions; they simply want to have a good time.

Apparently, audiences want what's familiar. When Jesse McKinley wrote in *The New York Times* about "*The Case of the Incredible Shrinking Blockbuster*" he articulately described how that turn-of-the-century juggernaut *The Producers* has been slowly dying over the years. *The Producers*, of course, is the much-praised musical based on the brilliant Mel Brooks film of the 1960s. And it was a smash from day one. It's a story audiences already knew and loved. And it was originally cast with two leading men who audiences also new and loved from both TV and motion-picture fame (Nathan Lane and Matthew Broderick).

But once that initial hype was gone—once those two celebrities left the Broadway production and were replaced with quite competent actors (although with little name recognition), the box office fell tremendously. The show did not even make it into the Top Ten for the week ending December 14, 2003. In fact, *The Producers* (in many theatrical circles) is often-times lovingly referred to as Broadway's great under-achiever.

And then the producers of *The Producers* eagerly announced the gallant return of Messrs Lane and Broderick for a limited run in early 2004, and the box office surged $3.6 million dollars.

Indeed. Let's give the audiences something familiar (*The Producers*) with two familiar celebrities (Lane and Broderick) once again. What an absolutely perfect no-risk combination!

Union vs Non-Union . . . that is the question!

With the costs of producing shows continually soaring to the heavens, producers are always eager to find new opportunities which will make their theatrical ventures more profitable. And so we've been seeing more and more producers making what some might consider to be quite daring decisions about how their future shows will be mounted.

It all began several years ago when the Disney organization

decided to bring their new stage musical *Beauty and the Beast* to New York's Palace Theatre. Instead of simply following the crowd—instead of producing their show the same way everyone else produces shows—the Disney folks determined it might be in their best interest if they didn't necessarily follow the rules, but rather *create* some of those rules themselves, specifically to address their own unique purposes.

Disney Theatricals had a long-term plan—to have two or even three productions running on Broadway in the not too distant future. They understood that with that great bargaining strength, they didn't necessarily have to accept the union agreements already in place—already established by the League of American Theatres and Producers (the IATSE Local 1 Agreement, in particular); rules which all Broadway producers simply follow and rarely question. So Disney decided to negotiate their *own* agreement, offering far better terms for the success of their productions.

And let's face it . . . the fact that Disney would have several shows playing simultaneously on Broadway—thereby offering the IATSE labor force (and others) numerous employment opportunities for many years to come—easily allowed the Disney organization to get their way. And today, they operate well within their own unique—and quite successful—world on Broadway.

But that's Disney; now, the real world. Without the massive power of the Disney organization behind them, independent producers and smaller production entities simply do not hold the same bargaining chip, and are therefore left to their own devises in order to make their operations more successful. And some of those producers have to work in a far different world—mounting their shows completely within a non-union structure.

Most of these productions of course are road companies; attempting this sort of strategy in the heavily unionized New

York City environment would not be the wisest move, I would think. Nonetheless, the mold has been broken, and non-union productions are now touring the country quite successfully.

In one way—this appears to be a win/win situation. Producers are able to engage a talented cast of performers and creative staff at a far lesser cost than they would have to endure with an Actor's Equity/SSDC (Society of Stage Directors and Choreographers) affiliation. And because of such savings, several of the shows with larger casts are able then to be sent out on the road with the full complement of cast members (some of those larger shows such as the official National Tour of *42ⁿᵈ Street* had to be scaled down to a smaller cast size; it just wouldn't be profitable using the actual number needed while working under a union agreement). Audiences then would be given the opportunity to see the *full complement* of performers as in the Broadway original, rather than a scaled-down/built-to-travel road version. And so— producers' costs are lessened; actors are employed; and audiences are happy. What more could anyone ask for?

Naturally, the theatrical unions are not pleased about this new and gathering development. Actor's Equity, in particular, has had a long battle with such non-union producers—Big League Theatricals, among others. The union position is that audiences around the country are being deceived because such producers employ "non-professional" talent on stage. They also openly protest the fact that their union members are being locked out of such employment opportunities since AEA has prohibited their membership from working within non-union productions. If caught, penalties could range from monetary fines, to full revocation of that union member's Equity Card.

No matter how much complaining the various unions might espouse on this matter, it is no doubt a problem that will not easily go away. It's a crisis they will have to face; have to resolve. Non-equity tours today are ubiquitous, and they will continue to thrive. The financials make the case. Actor's Equity and the SSD&C (and others) would be wise to sit with these independent producers and work out a deal—offering such producers the financial relief they need in order to make mounting such road shows financial viable, while still offering their union members the benefits (or at least *some* of the benefits) of union affiliation.

In a recent interview, the successful producer Cameron Mackintosh boasted of his record of never having to go "non-union" with any of his productions (*The Phantom of the Opera*, *Les Miserables*, *Miss Saigon*, *Oklahoma!*, etc.), while still being able to maintain top-notch production quality and a full cast complement. And he swears he never will.

I guess we'll all soon see if that will indeed be true in the difficult years to come.

It should be noted that British Actor's Equity has yet to see the union vs. non-union issue to the full extent that it currently exists in the United States. Perhaps—as most insiders would agree—it's because British Equity is not as strong a union as it's American counter-part. Nonetheless, the situation will no doubt raise its head rather soon. And I would think that the final result of this battle within the United States will most likely set the stage for a similar resolution in the United Kingdom as well.

On My Own

And finally, we must address a pandemic of unbearable sadness—one which has effected us all; one which none of us can escape.

The closing decades of the 20th century brought a terrific scourge upon the world—perhaps hitting Broadway and London's West End hardest of all. The onset of AIDS caused an entire generation to be lost. And with it went the irreplaceable skills of an invaluable team of theatrical innovators—producers, directors, choreographers, designers, actors, and theatrical managers too.

The devastation caused by AIDS is the missing link—the nexus, if you will—from one talented generation to the next—leaving few to carry-over the ever-evolving genius of theatrical creativity to the great stages of the world.

And so those theatrical linchpins are gone; the creative link between the close of the 20th century and on into the next, lost forever. In a way—today—we're starting over . . . fresh . . . with little, if any, connection to the continual evolution of theatrical creativity.

As is well implied by the clichéd aphorism "the blind leading the blind"—we're moving ahead. Slowly, yet moving ahead nonetheless. The destination, however, is yet to be determined.

Motive and Opportunity

There has been a renaissance of discussion in recent years about creating a National Theatre here in the United States not unlike Britain's Royal National Theatre. It would house a permanent acting company which would cull the finest offerings from the country's regional stages and present them in a beautifully-designed performing arts complex which was recently proposed by master architect Daniel Libeskind for a renewed World Trade Center site in lower Manhattan. This, in itself—is a wonderful idea.

Creating a National Theatre has long been a desire of writers and actors and theatre-goers for years. Indeed, Lincoln Center's Vivian Beaumont Theatre was first established with that mandate in mind, yet somehow got waylaid along the way.

Some believe Washington DC's The Kennedy Center for the Performing Arts already considers itself the nation's cultural center.

No doubt the idea of a National Theatre sounds great—let the government give producers all the money they need to produce shows. How perfect would that be?

Yet nothing is free—least of all, public funding. And as it is with investment on Broadway . . . when one (person or entity) is investing a good deal of money, I'm sure they will want a say in how that money will be spent.

Having the American government sponsor or support the arts in such a fashion is a fantasy which I believe will never see the light of day. It's simply not the American way.

And who, after all, would want the American government to influence or control theatrical content in any way, shape, or form?

"The significance of the theatre in society has been greatly reduced . . ."
—Arthur Miller

We're no doubt living in the age of information—information overload, if you will. The theatre is no longer needed to convey ideas or emotions. It is no longer needed to present political satire or social commentary. It is no longer needed to say very much of anything.

We all get our information in many different ways. 24-hour news services and the Internet have made us savvier, and far more aware. But we're passive receptors of that information; there's not much thinking needed. All is analyzed for us. Indeed, there's little for us to do.

Producers on both sides of the Atlantic seem to be developing a credo—Don't challenge the audience too much. Don't push them too far. And whatever you do, don't make them think.

And when productions like *Jerry Springer—The Opera* wins London's Evening Star Award as Best New Musical—and New

York producers are trampling over each other in a desperate attempt to secure that show's Broadway rights—it's no surprise then to see just how much the industry has changed.

Indeed—it seems the more an audience knows, the less they want to think. So be ready for such theatrical trends to well follow that need.

And so from where I sit, I'm afraid today's audiences are getting just what they're asking for; and perhaps just what they deserve.

Appendix A

Why Can't I Get Tickets?

A REPORT ON TICKET DISTRIBUTION PRACTICES

BUREAU OF INVESTOR PROTECTION AND SECURITIES

MAY 27, 1999

EXECUTIVE SUMMARY

"The process by which tickets wend their way from the original issuer to the ultimate consumer is complex and often illegal. In the general case, the consumer walks up to the box office or telephones a ticket agent such as Telecharge or Ticketmaster (or uses one of their outlets), pays the price on the face of the ticket (with perhaps a small additional service charge) and obtains the ticket that he or she wants. Too often, however, the consumer finds that the desired ticket (e.g. to *The Lion King* or the Yankee playoffs or the Spice Girls) is unavailable within minutes after it goes on sale, and if there are any tickets left, they are at the rear of the house, the highest tier of the stadium or, in the case of a hit show, the wait can be for over a year. However, while a "sold-out" sign confronts the consumer at the box office, the newspapers nonetheless are filled with advertisements for the most sought after seats—at prices, depending on the popularity of the event, ranging into the thousands of dollars. The Attorney General's investigation demonstrates that ticket distribution practices are seriously skewed away from ordinary fans and towards wealthy businesses and consumers.

This problem is not simply the result of the law of supply and demand. Rather, the availability of tickets and the outrageously high—and illegal—prices that brokers charge, to a large extent, can be laid at the door of illicit practices in the ticket industry and other practices that, although possibly not unlawful, are deceptive, unfair to the ticket buying public and supportive of the corrupt ticket distribution system.

Thus, the average disappointed consumer walks away with the suspicion that the tickets could not have all been sold, through the normal means, quite that fast. He or she often believes that someone, somewhere, had an "in," and that dutifully waiting on line or telephoning repeatedly was, in reality, an exercise in futility. To a large extent, that frustrated consumer is correct. This report attempts to explain why and highlights the myths, half truths, and outright criminality that causes the scarcity of tickets.

The entertainment industry is one of the core sources of revenue for New York. Just as we demand integrity of New York's financial institutions and its securities marketplace, New Yorkers have a right to expect integrity in the system through which tickets are distributed. New York's citizens and the millions of tourists who come to New York to attend entertainment and sporting events deserve to obtain tickets through a distribution system free of fraud and corruption.

A system that provides access to quality seating on the basis of bribes and corruption at the expense of the fans, without whose continued support the theatre could not survive, should not be tolerated. Indeed, Billy Joel stated in a recent interview that he would in fact stop doing live concerts because the system did not permit the "real fans" access to tickets.

He announced that he was going to stop touring in part because "I am tired of being part of the rip-off. The brokers that drive the prices up are ripping me off because, I'm not getting the money . . . and they're ripping off the customer because the customer wants the ticket and they know that the market will bear a certain price."

The price that tickets to popular events command in the marketplace belongs to the performers, producers and investors who create the events, not the speculators who through illegality and deception take advantage of the excess demand in the system. Ticket scalping is sometimes referred to as a "victimless" crime. To the contrary, the victims of the current ticket distribution system are the fans, the producers and investors who create the events and the State of New York, which loses both tax revenues and credibility as the entertainment center of the world.

The facts and analysis set forth below have been collected through activities of the Attorney General's Office, including:

   *   The issuance of over 200 subpoenas for documents and testimony, 40% which were to New York ticket brokers (many asserted the privilege against self-incrimination; several failed to substantially comply with the subpoena), and concierges of nine major New York City hotels;
   *   The taking of testimony from or interviews of owners and management of major venues, representatives of ticketing agencies, concert promoters, group sales and theatre party agents, venue security personnel, clients of ticket brokers, business associates of ticket brokers, various state and city officials, and a number of confidential informants;

*   The prosecution and conviction of the treasurer of the Jones Beach Marine Theatre on charges of larceny and computer tampering, and the trial of the owners of a ticket brokerage firm for ticket speculation;

*   The execution of search warrants at two New York and two New Jersey ticket brokerage firms;

*   The review of the records of six Broadway productions—at least one in each of New York's three major theatre chains—as well as those of a major not-for-profit theatre;

*   The examination of computer print-outs of nine major concerts at Madison Square Garden and the Nassau Coliseum, as well as the computer print-outs of all 37 concerts at the Jones Beach Marine Theatre in the summer of 1996;

*   The review of subscription records for the Knicks and Rangers, and the United States Open ticket sales for 1997;

*   Comparison of tickets purchased or seized from ticket brokers and scalpers against records of venues;

*   Surveys of ticket holders at the June 20-23, 1994 Barbra Streisand concerts at Madison Square Garden; the August 4, 1996 Hootie and the Blowfish concert, and the August 17, 1996 Alanis Morrisette concert at the Jones Beach Marine Theatre; and the July 1, 1998 Spice Girls concert at Madison Square Garden;

*   Visits to over a dozen locations such as Ticketmaster outlets, entertainment venues, and ticket brokers.

In addition to addressing the endemic corruption in the ticket business through his criminal and civil enforcement powers, the Attorney General believes that nothing will change until the public knows how the system works and new legislation is enacted. Legislative and policy recommendations flow from this investigation, and are intended to improve the availability of entertainment tickets to consumers, as well as provide new powers to fight the illegal conduct. This report is intended to promote that process.

A. Corrupt Practices

Ticket brokers strive to monopolize the supply of tickets by paying illegal and substantial bribes (premiums over the face price of the ticket) to various persons who have control over tickets at the original point of sale. These persons with control over tickets include box office employees or their supervisors, managers of venues, ticketing agents (such as employees of Ticketmaster or Telecharge), concert promoters, security personnel, or a variety of house seat holders. The pay-offs made to a venue operator, agent or employee, (e.g., a box office employee), is historically known as "ice".

Ticket brokers must be licensed pursuant to New York's Arts and Cultural Affairs Law ("ACAL"). Under ACAL, the payment or receipt of ice is currently a crime, classified as a misdemeanor, and also subjects a ticket seller to revocation or suspension of his or her registration as a ticket distributor. Payments of premiums to individuals other than agents of the venue (such as promoters and house seat holders) are not specifically covered by ACAL, but can be covered by other provisions of the criminal law, such as commercial bribery. Such payments are hard to prove. They are almost always made in cash, not necessarily at the recipient's place of business, and generally occur between two people, without witnesses.

Brokers who pay ice must of course cover the cost of the bribe, which can range from 50 to 100 percent of the face price of the ticket. Therefore, they have to resell tickets substantially above the current legal maximum of an additional five dollars or ten percent of the face price (whichever is greater), and cannot operate within any reasonable cap. As such, these tickets are sold illegally, generally by out-of-state brokers to New York businesses —such as securities firms that need tickets for clients. One major New York securities firm paid a New Jersey broker over $360,000 during 1994 to obtain for itself the finest seats at various venues, at clearly illegal prices, ranging from 150 to 600 percent above the face value of each ticket.

B. Unfair Practices

Aside from ice and bribery, huge numbers of tickets for popular events are diverted from sale to the public and are distributed through other channels. The extent to which tickets are channeled through this non-public system, and the persons and businesses that get their tickets through "connections," are subjects that have been shrouded in secrecy for many years. Whether in connection with illegal payments or not, the sheer number of seats withheld from public sale lends itself to manipulation and abuse. Such tickets are almost always the best seats in the house. Tickets set aside for theatre party or group sales agents wind up being resold by ticket brokers; house seats at theatres make up a great part of the ticket broker's stock in trade, as do tickets set aside by concert promoters.

Moreover, the failure of venues adequately to inform the public—as to the number and location of seats available for public sale, the date on which a new batch of seats for a show or concert might go on sale, or when un-purchased house seats become available to the public—goes hand-in-hand with the practices set forth above. For example, during the 1994 Barbra Streisand concerts at Madison Square Garden, approximately 50 percent of the seats never went on public sale, i.e., they were withheld for the "house"—the producer, the promoter, the record company, the performer, or other such individuals. Had this been disclosed to the public in the advertising for the event, the public would have had more realistic expectations about their chances of obtaining a ticket through general sales. The Attorney General believes that most consumers would be surprised to learn that for most events, a very large percentage of all seats and most of the best seats for a particular event are in reality unavailable to the public.

C. The De Facto Framework

Ticket brokers converge just outside of New York's borders—some, just minutes away—to advertise and sell tickets to New Yorkers but generally claim—incorrectly—that they are not subject to New York laws. Box office employees and former box office employees either have special relationships with ticket brokers and scalpers or, eliminating the "middle man" entirely, are ticket brokers themselves. Concert promoters or their affiliates are also ticket brokers. And law enforcement is left to combat the problems of ticket diversion and commercial bribery with inadequate and outdated weapons.

Meanwhile, as more fully described in this report, insiders have little incentive to change the situation. The theatre and arena owners receive their flat fee rents and percentage of the gross no matter how or to whom the tickets are sold. Equally unaffected by ticket sales practices are the producers, promoters and star performers who receive a negotiated percentage of the gross. Group sales agents and licensed New York ticket brokers also do a substantial business with their respective share of the action. The latter group settles, by and large, for the hotel tourist trade and the less desirable seats. They work with unlicensed brokers, assisting them in "laying off" some of the risk of being left with unsold tickets. New York corporations and businesses have the ability to obtain the best seats on short notice for their clients and associates. The reason there are no good seats available at box office prices for the fans of New York sports teams or for the U.S. Open tennis matches is because, as the insiders say, they have all "gone corporate." The same is true for concerts. This has created a two-class system for access to sports and entertainment events.

Where, therefore, is the incentive for anyone in the business of sports and entertainment to change the system? Fans and theatre lovers—those without special contacts or influence—often turn to the Attorney General's Office for help.

D. How Illegal Brokers Get Tickets

How tickets wind up in the lucrative resale market rather than in the hands of fans is one of the subjects of this report. The following is a summary of the methods by which ticket brokers acquire tickets—those they are willing to talk about, as well as the corrupt methods they are not willing to acknowledge.

1. The Acknowledged Methods

There are various methods by which ticket brokers claim to obtain their product legally.

* Brokers send "diggers" to stand on line at the box office.
* Brokers use high-speed dialing equipment and other methods to increase their chance of getting through by the telephone.
* Brokers buy tickets, for a legal premium, from fans who have been able to buy tickets.
* Brokers send in numerous mail orders for Broadway shows, generally in the individual names of employees or of surrogates, such as family and friends.

2. The Unacknowledged Methods

The Attorney General's investigation has uncovered illegal or corrupt methods by which ticket brokers consistently obtain the best seats to the most popular events in quantities that belie the "acknowledged" explanations as to their source.

*   Brokers obtain seats from promoters, performers and representatives of venues (including box office treasurers and ticket sellers) by paying ice. In some instances, box office personnel have ownership interests in ticket brokers or have family members who are ticket brokers.

*   Brokers obtain tickets from computer ticketing companies such as Ticketmaster, whose employees are skimming tickets for themselves and selling them to brokers (or from distant outlets less likely to have a great demand for a show in New York City). When additional dates are added for a performance for which there is a great demand, they may not be advertised, thus creating the opportunity for outlet operators to advise their "friends" when the additional tickets will go on sale. In one instance, a small video store with a Ticketmaster terminal is silently owned by a New Jersey ticket broker.

*   Brokers obtain from the box office "house seats" that are not used by those persons entitled to use the house seats or that are held for performances at which such seats are released for theatre parties or large groups, or they obtain seats which were set aside for other promotional or marketing purposes (e.g., special agreements with credit card companies to hold a certain number of "best seats" for their gold or platinum card holders).

Brokers also buy from each other. One may have a "hook" (a contact) at one venue, others may have different "hooks." Thus, there is a constant stream of faxes flowing between them showing the tickets available. As a result of the variety of contacts or "hooks" among ticket brokers, different brokers tend to become known as specializing in certain events (e.g., Knicks and Rangers, *The Phantom of the Opera*, etc.) Actually, this "specialization" is nothing more than having a "hook" with whom a broker can transact illegal business.

Members of the organized ticket broker industry basically have one answer to the question of how they get their tickets: the use of "diggers." While they resist discussing the issue of the source of their supply, if pressed they almost always say that they send "diggers" to stand on line at the box office or, less frequently, that they buy from original purchasers or have techniques for getting in on the telephone. This answer begs the question of how the brokers obtain the best seats in the house—the seats commanding huge prices and demanded by the brokers' business clientele, who expect large volume service on short notice—in such large quantities.

In addition, diggers always seem to get the scarce number of high quality tickets available at the box office while the real fans are left "in the cold." Many such fans have called the Attorney General's Office to complain about and describe the chaotic scene outside a venue when numbered wrist-bands (presumably instituted to assure fairness) are distributed a day before or hours before an "on-sale." Fans also complain about standing on line or camping-out for hours, if not days, to buy tickets for concerts, just to be told that all tickets are sold out or that the best seats are not available because they are reserved for the "fan club" or "VIPS." Diggers however, somehow manage to buy seats that are not available to the fans.

E. Policy and Law

This is a huge business. Hundreds of ticket resellers who work out of offices, not on the street, make a substantial living from it, indeed, become wealthy from it, as do many of their suppliers at the original point of sale. The statutes we have to deal with this system are holdovers from a bygone era. The Attorney General's investigation has highlighted several shortcomings in the existing law that ought to be remedied, as well as policies and rules that should be adopted by the industry. Following is a summary of these:

* The payment and receipt of ice, currently a misdemeanor if prosecuted under Article 25 of ACAL, should be a felony to provide a greater deterrent against such activity.

* The diversion of tickets from public sale to ticket brokers by employees or agents of a venue, without the express authorization of the owner or operator of the venue or of the producer or promoter, should be illegal even without proof of bribery.

* Currently the resale of one ticket for over the "maximum premium price" (the face price on the ticket plus five dollars or ten percent of the face price, whichever is greater) is a violation under ACAL; the resale of five or more tickets is a misdemeanor, whether as an isolated event or as part of the business of reselling tickets. The sale of 20 or more tickets or tickets in an amount totaling more than $1,000 over the statutory limit should be a Class E felony, similar to a larceny when the value of stolen property exceeds $1,000.

* The statutory cap on the price of tickets should be raised to permit licensed ticket brokers who do not pay bribes to make a reasonable profit.

* The identity of the individual ticket seller should be ascertainable either by requiring an identifying code printed on the face of the ticket or by requiring such identification to be retained in the computer.

* The ticket broker business is no longer conducted in a particular county, on the street or in an office, as when the law was written, but by telephone, fax and computer on a state-wide and inter-state basis. Therefore, centralized, state-wide licensing and other provisions reflecting the current state of the ticket resale business should be enacted.

    *   The investigation and enforcement provisions of the ticket resale law are currently inadequate to deal with the systemic corruption that underpins the ticket resale business. Civil and criminal penalties must be increased so that they are no longer seen as just a potential cost of doing business.

    *   The secrecy surrounding current ticket distribution practices should be lifted. The law should provide for increased disclosure as to the availability of tickets to the ultimate consumer.

    *   Ticket resale and the related payment of bribes to insiders has become part of a large underground economy that is depriving New York of lawful income and sales tax. Undeclared taxable income received by box office employees and others is a matter requiring increased enforcement activity. Requiring the payment of sales tax on the amount of the resale ticket price above the face price of the ticket must be expressly enacted into law.

    *   Consideration should be given to prohibiting the purchase of 20 or more tickets over a specified period of time for over the maximum premium price.

This report focuses not just on ticket scalping, but also on how tickets get from their original point of distribution to the resale market where they command such unconscionable and illegal prices, and how to assure increased access to tickets at reasonable prices to the large majority of the public who support, by their continued interest and enthusiasm, New York sports and entertainment events. The Attorney General's investigation into the institutionalized system of fraud and corruption surrounding the ticket distribution system is continuing. It is the hope of the Attorney General that the findings and recommendations discussed below will trigger corrective actions that could be taken now.

II. AN OVERVIEW OF THE TICKET RESALE BUSINESS AND THE GOVERNING LAW

A. Ticket Scalpers, Ticket Brokers — Premium and Non-Premium and Dump Houses

"Ticket scalping" has been embodied in the popular culture as an activity that generally takes place on the street, frequently in front of or near the venue for which tickets are being sold. Because of public safety concerns resulting from many people milling around event sites attempting to buy and sell tickets, the New York State legislature prohibited ticket resales within 1,000 feet of the property line of places of entertainment having a permanent seating capacity in excess of 5,000 seats, unless the operator has designated an area for resale of tickets that are not usable by the purchaser.(1) Street scalpers are, however, the smallest part of the immense ticket resale industry.(2)

The ticket resale industry in New York is by and large divided into those ticket brokers who operate and obtain licenses in New York(3) and those who do business in New York(4) but maintain that they do not do business in New York because they are located on the immediate outskirts of New York.(5) Places like Union City and Fort Lee, New Jersey, which are 15 minute drives from Broadway, are extremely popular with ticket brokers who sell tickets to New York events to New York residents.(6)

This distinction is, however, not set in concrete, but made only to serve as convenient shorthand for purposes of explication and discussion.(7) Some out-of-state ticket broker firms obtain licenses in New York. Other out-of-state ticket brokers own or are affiliated with New York ticket brokers and direct the bulk, if not all, of their seats to an unlicensed out-of-state affiliate. New

York ticket broker firms, licensed and unlicensed, operate outside the law, sometimes flagrantly so. In addition, there are many formal and informal connections between New York and out-of-state ticket brokers and between those resellers who are colorably operating within the law(8) and those who are blatantly outside it.

In the group colorably within the law are ticket brokers with offices in New York City and concession desks in many New York City hotels.(9) They deal primarily in Broadway theatre tickets and their clients are frequently tourists to New York. Such brokers are licensed, charge anywhere between ten and over 60 percent above the face price of a Broadway theatre ticket and generally do not obtain the most desirable seats.(10) Resellers in this group are, therefore, generally referred to as "non-premium" brokers.(11) They may also be referred to as "dump houses" because some of the major ones assist the premium brokers by allowing the latter to lay off or "dump" expensive, about to expire, tickets that they would otherwise be left holding. Non-premium brokers argue that they are an essential part of the New York theatrical business because they actually help keep many marginal shows running by reselling their tickets to a largely tourist trade.

Non-premium brokers justify their mark-ups—a clear violation of the law—as "service" charges (which Article 25 does not expressly address) and as a necessary cost of doing business.(12)

In contrast to the non-premium brokers are those that are unlicensed and operating outside New York. Also known as "premium brokers," they are primarily distinguishable from the former group because they can generally obtain the most desirable seats or "hot" tickets on short notice and their primary clients are New York businesses such as stock brokerage firms, fashion and publishing industry companies, and advertising, law and accounting firms.(13) For such clients, money seems to be no object. Many have running accounts with out-of-state ticket resellers and their charges for tickets run into tens of thousands of dollars. For instance, during 1994 alone, a New York securities firm paid Herman Agar, Co., a New Jersey ticket broker, $367,980.99 for such tickets. See Exhibit B.

Mark-ups taken by premium brokers range from approximately 130 percent to over 450 percent. For example, on average, a $75 or $80 orchestra seat to a Broadway musical in New York City will be sold for between $100 to $110 by a licensed broker and for $175 by a premium broker. Tickets with a face price of $350 for the 1994 Barbara Streisand concerts at Madison Square Garden in New York City were being sold by premium brokers for prices as high as $2000. In the summer of 1995, $50 tickets for the Melissa Etheridge concert at Jones Beach, on Long Island, were selling for $450, and $50 tickets for R.E.M. at Madison Square Garden were selling for $350. In the summer of 1998, a ticket to the U.S. Open women's semi-final with a face price of $85 was being offered by SRO Entertainment for between $1700 and $2000.

A phenomenon clearly on the rise is the offer and resale of tickets by ticket brokers over the Internet. While purchasing tickets via the Internet may be more convenient for the consumer—it is easier to shop around for locations and prices—it does not change the basic structure of the ticket resale business. Ticket brokers must still obtain their supply of tickets at the original source and, whether by advertising in the New York media or sending an Internet transmission to a New York purchaser, they still subject themselves to New York law, since New York's jurisdiction is based upon whether the buyer or seller is located in New York. A recent survey of such sales found the following postings,(14) with bids expected to rise:

Event	Face Value	Bid on Ebay on 4/19/99
New York Yankees at New York Mets Friday, July 9; section 37, two tickets	$20	$152.50
New York, Mets at New York Yankees Saturday June 5; Field box section 21 two tickets.	$100	$300
The Lion King on Broadway, May 28; third-row orchestra seats, three tickets.	$225	$505
Miami Heat at New York Knicks May 5; section 223, two tickets.	$130	$227.51
Atlanta Braves at New York Yankees July 15; lower level, main club box 250, four tickets.	$150	$355

A new potential use of the Internet and one that may have more far reaching effects on the business of selling and reselling tickets involves the online-auction sites of concert artists.(15) Several artists are expected to begin auctioning tickets online in the summer of 1999. In fact, during the summer of 1998, concert performers Jimmy Page and Robert Plant auctioned 50 premium seats for their tour on Best Buy Online and gave the proceeds to charity. Of course, offering or selling tickets for over the maximum premium price to New York purchasers violates New York law. However, such sales are currently occurring and artists and promoters "clearly . . . realize the need to get in on the action."(16)

As discussed in the Policy and Legislative Issues Section, infra, excess profits in the system should benefit venues and creators of entertainment events:

The problem for artists and venues is that scalping takes money out of their pockets. This has always been the case with offline scalpers, but Web auctions offer a chance to level the playing field. The popularity of online scalping is forcing the industry to concede that there's a viable secondary market online.(17)

Currently, however, such "leveling of the playing field" is against the law. Whether the law can accommodate the entry of these new resellers over the Internet is an issue that the legislature should undoubtedly address.

B. Distinction Between Primary And Secondary Market

A ticket, the right of entry to a particular event, is originally issued by either the venue where the event will take place or by its producer. It is either physically produced in the form of a hard piece of paper or, if admission to an event is to be sold through a computer ticketing system, said seats will be entered into a computer program containing the exact number of seats, dates and locations available for sale to the public. In either case, tickets placed on the market are issued by the venue, and such venue is the "original ticket seller." The original or initial sale of the ticket may occur in a variety of ways: at the box office in person, by telephone, by mail or through a computer ticketing company such as Ticketmaster by telephone or at an outlet.

The role played by computer ticketing companies such as Ticketmaster and Telecharge has been a source of confusion. These companies serve the venue by providing the computer technology and the distribution system for ticket sales. As such, they are agents of the venue. As a matter of practice, these companies make their money by adding a fee to the price of each ticket, agreed upon with the venue, for their service in processing and distributing the ticket. While there has been much argument that these fees are too high, they should be distinguished from the charges added by ticket brokers and ticket scalpers upon the resale of a ticket. So-called "processing fees" may also be charged by a venue itself for the use of a credit card or for telephone processing.

Only after the ticket has been sold at the point of an original sale—whether at a box office or by a computer ticketing agent at an outlet—at the face price (plus a possible processing or computer company service fee if applicable), can the ticket be resold on the secondary market by a broker or scalper. This is where huge, sometimes extraordinary, mark-ups come into the picture.

C. Relationships Between Ticket Sellers and Ticket Brokers

All ticket brokers are not created equal. Aside from the obvious factor of size—ranging from the large ticket resale business with annual gross receipts in the millions of dollars to the street scalper with a handful of illicitly acquired tickets—certain resellers have access to certain venues where they have a "hook". Frequently, this hook is based on a familial relationship or an acquaintanceship based on prior working relationships in a particular box office.(18) In any event, certain resellers are able to obtain the most desirable tickets to certain venues and not others. Some resellers are "hooked" into certain Broadway shows; other resellers specialize in certain sporting events; yet others specialize in concerts. Nevertheless, large resellers have to provide a full-service operation for their large and demanding business clientele, as opposed to street scalpers who hawk what they have when they have it. Therefore, there is a great deal of inter-dependency and trade between ticket resellers. This is accomplished by a constant exchange of faxes, in which resellers advise each other on a daily basis of the tickets they have in inventory. See Exhibits C through E.

D. The Governing Law: Arts and Cultural Affairs Law, Articles 23 and 25.

The original sale of a ticket to any "place of entertainment" in New York is governed by sections 23.23 and 25.29 of ACAL.

Section 23.23 of ACAL creates the regulatory framework for the original sale of tickets at the box office. It provides for the registration as a "ticket distributor" of all owners, operators or operating lessees of places of entertainment, as defined in § 23.03(1)(i), and their agents, representatives and employees, including box office employees who at any time have control of the allocation or distribution of tickets. Any individual named on a "ticket distribution registration" is subject to an order canceling or suspending that registration or an order barring him or her from selling tickets when he or she has participated in receiving any premium in excess of the established price of the ticket ("ice") or any practice operating as a fraud upon the public or amounting to financial misconduct.

ACAL § 25.29 is the criminal counterpart of § 23.23(4). It provides that any operator of a place of entertainment or his or her agent, representative or employee, who receives a premium in excess of the established price (ice) shall be guilty of a misdemeanor punishable by a fine not to exceed $500, or by a term of imprisonment not to exceed one year, or both. See ACAL §§ 25.29, 25.35.

Except as discussed above, ACAL Article 25 deals with the resale of tickets.(19) It provides the statutory framework governing the resale of tickets and the resellers of tickets, as opposed to the original sale of tickets and original sellers of tickets primarily regulated by ACAL § 23.23. The primary mechanisms created by Article 25 require ticket resellers to be licensed with the commissioner of licenses of the political subdivision in which such business is conducted (e.g.,the Department of Consumer Affairs in New York City, hereinafter the "Department"); require places of entertainment to print the established price on the face of each ticket; and prohibit the resale of tickets for over the "maximum premium price," currently defined in § 25.03(4) as five dollars or ten percent of the established price, whichever is greater. In addition, § 25.25 requires licensees to keep records of the names and addresses of all persons from whom tickets were purchased and to whom they were sold, and the price at which such transactions occurred. These records must be made available to the Attorney General upon request.

E. The Relationship Between Ticket Scalping and Corruption in the Box Office

The Attorney General has concluded that one of the primary reasons for the inflated prices on the resale market is that certain brokers have to cover the cost of payments of ice. Ice is money paid, in the form of a gratuity, premium or bribe, in excess of the printed box office price of a ticket, to an operator of any place of entertainment or such operator's agent, representative or employee.(20) Box office employees and their supervisors who control the original sale and distribution of tickets are such agents. There can be no meaningful discussion or analysis of the ticket resale(21) business without considering the impact that ice has on that business.

Premium ticket brokers or sellers, discussed above, need access to large quantities of the best seats to the most desirable events on short notice in order to keep and satisfy their demanding client base. Such tickets cannot be obtained by standing on line or by paying diggers to stand on line, nor can premium brokers rely on getting through on telephone lines (even with sophisticated speed-dialing equipment). They must have an advantage. That advantage is derived by paying ice, sometimes in amounts that almost equal the face price of the ticket.

Joseph Nekola, the treasurer of the Jones Beach Marine Theatre box office was paid $ 20-25 over the face price for each ticket he diverted to brokers for Jones Beach concerts.(22) As one representative of a theatre acknowledged to a member of the Attorney General's staff, box office employees think of ice as both a gratuity and an entitlement; it represents the major source of illegally obtained tickets. As discussed infra in Section III, investigating and proving the payment of ice has been a challenge faced by the Attorney General's Office for years and the complaints about access to events did not always involve popular groups like the Spice Girls or Metallica.

For example, in January 1978, the great classical pianist Vladimir Horowitz was returning to play in New York after a long absence. Carnegie Hall advertised that 2500 hundred seats for the concert would be sold to the public commencing at 9:00 a.m. on the day of the sale. Horowitz aficionados started lining up to buy tickets the night before. It was a cold night and there were elderly people on the line. Using New York ingenuity, someone in the line obtained a roll of numbered tickets from a local store and assigned numbers to the waiting fans so that they could temporarily leave the line. As a result of this system, it became evident that the 2500 advertised tickets were not, in fact, available for purchase by the general public because when the "sold-out" sign went up, only 1900 tickets had been sold.

A group of disappointed Horowitz fans complained to the Attorney General's Office. The result of the ensuing investigation was the finding that the 600 missing tickets had, indeed, been set aside with the knowledge of management. The General Manager and Assistant General Manager of Carnegie Hall signed Assurances of Discontinuance.

F. Maximum Premium Price

The "maximum premium price" provision of New York law has become one of the "hot button" issues among ticket brokers and the lobbyists who represent them in Albany and in Trenton. The "maximum premium price" under current New York law is "the sum of the established price plus five dollars or ten percent of the established price, whichever is greater, plus lawful taxes."(23)

The maximum premium price is almost universally disregarded by ticket resellers. Nevertheless, ticket resellers, particularly those outside of New York, have mounted a strenuous campaign to convince the New York legislature to repeal the maximum premium price provision of ACAL regulating the ticket resale price (i.e., the secondary market price). This campaign has borrowed the high-minded phrase "free market" from economic theory in a totally inappropriate way, since monopolizing the supply of tickets at their original source through criminal activity hardly qualifies as free market activity.(24)

A bill supported by the East Coast Ticket Brokers Association ("ECTBA") was introduced in New York in 1995.(25) The argument made in support of the bill was that if the maximum premium price were repealed, ECTBA's members would move back to New York (although no evidence has been presented that they moved away from New York) and pay taxes in New York; and that as a result of free market forces, the price of tickets on the resale or secondary market would decrease. These are the same arguments that were made to convince the New Jersey legislature to repeal its ticket resale law in 1995. As discussed below, none of the promised benefits were realized and the "free market" experiment was abandoned after 18 months.

G. The New Jersey "Free Market" Experiment

New Jersey's ticket resale law(26) covers only tickets to New Jersey events. That is why ticket brokers who sell tickets to New York events to New York purchasers operate their businesses in out-of-state places such as Fort Lee, New Jersey (just across the George Washington Bridge). While these brokers attempt to take advantage of the gap created by the lack of uniformity between New York and New Jersey law by placing themselves physically outside New York's reach, the courts have clearly upheld New York's jurisdiction in such cases.

With respect to New Jersey events, New Jersey law prohibits brokers from charging over three dollars or 20 per cent, which-ever is greater, above the ticket face price. In 1995, New Jersey adopted a law removing the price cap on all entertainment tick-ets for a period of 18 months, so that the legislature could assess "whether lifting the resale price caps makes more tickets available to consumers at prices lower than those now charged by unli-censed resellers."(27) The New Jersey Attorney General and New Jersey Director of Consumer Affairs provided Governor Chris-tine Todd Whitman with an assessment of this 18-month moratorium. This report called into question, among other things, the reliability of data supplied by ECTBA, and it stated that "the brokers compare apples and oranges with regard to venues." For instance, as to the brokers' claims that ticket prices had fallen, the report stated that "if anything, [the information] points to op-posite conclusions from those reached by the brokers."(28)

Similarly, claims of lower prices had been made by the brokers for bands such as Metallica, that did not even appear in New Jersey during the moratorium period. The report concluded that: [T]here is no definite link between the moratorium and ticket availability or price. Moreover the Divisions own experiences . . . lead to the conclusion that there is no factual support for the assertion that prices fell or supply increased because of the moratorium.

The Attorney General supports an increase in the "maximum premium price" in order to cover the actual business expenses of licensed brokers, as well as a reasonable profit. See Legislative Recommendations, Section VI, B infra. The maximum premium price, however, should not be so large as to cover the institutionalized bribery represented by the payment of ice to original ticket distributors.

III. HOW TICKETS MOVE FROM THE PRIMARY MARKET TO THE SECONDARY (RESALE) MARKET

A. Open Purchases by Illegal Brokers

In the category of information that is "hidden in plain sight" is the evidence provided by the records of numerous venues examined by the Attorney General's Office. Those records demonstrate that the venues are either openly selling tickets to illegal brokers or to individuals associated with illegal brokers as principals or employees. Although the Attorney General's investigation has not yet concluded, an examination of the records of venues such as the Arthur Ashe Tennis Stadium, Madison Square Garden, Radio City Music Hall, Disney's New Amsterdam Theatre, The Ford Center of the Performing Arts, Shubert's Majestic Theatre, Nederlander's Palace Theatre, Jujamcyn's Eugene O'Neil Theatre and of group sales agents has disclosed the purchasers who are affiliated with illegal brokers. This, despite the avowed official policy of each of the above venues either not to sell to unlicensed brokers or, as in the case of the United States Tennis Association and Madison Square Garden, not to sell to brokers at all.

When evidence of sales to brokers, directly or through associated individuals, was presented to the venues, licensed group sales agents and ticketing services, they had a consistent, across-the-board response—that they cannot be responsible for vetting every individual purchaser to determine whether purchase is occurring on behalf of a broker. Ticketmaster's procedure with respect to *The Lion King* tickets was to sell, by telephone, up to 19 tickets per performance for an unlimited number of performances in one transaction (i.e., one phone call). Thus, there were telephone transactions that involved the purchase of hundreds of tickets. While telephone operators and the personnel that handle mail orders may not be able to recognize the names of principals and employees of illegal, unlicensed ticket brokers, transactions of the magnitude documented below should have raised a red flag that the callers were ticket brokers. Similarly, as discussed more fully below, records reviewed by the Attorney General's Office show single individuals as the purchasers of multiple season subscriptions to sporting events—another circumstance that should have been more closely examined.

Of course, selling large numbers of tickets or season subscriptions to the same individual (even ticket brokers) is in and of itself not against the law, unless someone at the original point of distribution has received ice. However, the fact that venues do this supports the public's conclusion that average fans cannot get fair access to events at affordable prices, and is inconsistent with the stated policy of many venues not to sell to brokers. For example:

* Disney's *The Lion King*

A review of documents produced during our investigation disclosed that twenty-six individuals known to be ticket brokers or affiliated with ticket brokers purchased *The Lion King* tickets in quantities of two and three hundred or more through the Ticketmaster phone center during the period of June 1, 1997 to December 29, 1997. Exhibit G. Others, who have not yet been identified as affiliates, had the same buying patterns.(29)

* The Shubert Organization's *The Phantom of the Opera*

In connection with a review of ticket sales for *The Phantom of the Opera* in 1994, the Shubert Organization provided the Attorney General with a list of the brokers who receive weekly allocations of tickets. Six of these brokers—Manhattan Entertainment, Greens Theatre Ticket Service (which appears to be affiliated with Herman Agar Co., a major, unlicensed New Jersey ticket broker), Jacobs Tickets, Turf Tickets, Hickey's Tickets and ABC Tickets—together, received 25 percent of the "best" seats (first 14 rows, center orchestra), for Friday and Saturday nights. Although the stated policy of the Shubert Organization is to do business only with bonded and licensed brokers, three of the above six ticket brokers are unlicensed and New Jersey based, including Herman Agar Co., Manhattan Entertainment and Jacobs Tickets, among the biggest (in terms of sales volume) ticket brokers in the tri-state area.

* The Nederlander Organization's *Beauty and the Beast* and Jujamcyn Theatres' *Grease*

Five of the six above-mentioned brokers plus two others — Original R'Tyson and See-More—received the house seats for

Beauty and the Beast and *Grease* according to 1994 records.(30) These seven brokers, along with two others—Capri and Rubin Ace (which is affiliated with Sherlock Tickets in Connecticut) also generally received the "best" seats, as defined above. Thus, nine ticket brokers always received the best seats to three of the most popular Broadway musicals in 1994 (the tenth, Jacobs Tickets, only received *The Phantom of the Opera* tickets), whereas New York non-premium brokers,(31) which did business with the same theatres, never received the best seats. Of the above mentioned brokers, three—Hickey's Tickets, Capri and Rubin Ace—failed to comply with a subpoena issued by the Attorney General in 1994. The owner of another Richard Markowitz of Original R' Tyson refused to testify, invoking the Fifth Amendment protection against self incrimination. In addition, the Attorney General's Office was involved in extended litigation with Herman Agar, Co. and Manhattan Entertainment, Inc. subsequent to its execution of search warrants (in cooperation with the New Jersey Attorney General) at their New Jersey premises.

* The Roundabout Theatre's *Cabaret*

The Roundabout Theatre, a respected not-for-profit theatre organization, found itself with a major musical hit during the 1997-1998 season: *Cabaret*. It came to the attention of the Attorney General that the Roundabout organization was openly selling tickets to ticket brokers, predominantly unlicensed, instead of the general public for between five and 25 dollars over the established or face price. The stated rationale for this apparent example of ice that was given to the Attorney General's Office was that these tickets were being sold as a package that included a souvenir T-shirt or a baseball cap. See Exhibit I.

* The United States Open

Although members of the public were unable to purchase any but the last two rows of seats to the 1997 U.S. Open by as early as April 1997, major unlicensed ticket brokers were able to acquire large amounts of tickets (some for the entire event, i.e. season tickets) in May, June, July and August of 1997 from the box office, despite the United States National Tennis Center's stated policy not to sell to ticket brokers.(32)

B. The Use of Surrogate Purchasers by Ticket Brokers

In a similar method designed to obtain large quantities of high quality tickets, brokers use surrogates and their credit cards. It has come to the attention of the Attorney General that a particular ticket broker uses dozens of different credit cards—cards in the names of family, friends, associates and other enlistees. In one instance, the attorney for the owner of an unlicensed New Jersey broker purchased $15,177 worth of concert and sporting event tickets on behalf of the broker. He was one of eight people who were used in this enterprise. Ticket brokers and their affiliated purchasers claim that they are simply more adept than members of the public at getting through on the telephone because of their greater efforts (e.g., they pay closer attention to news as to when new tickets are going on sale, they use speed dialing and other techniques). Diehard fans obviously dispute this claim.

C. Ice and Corruption

The Attorney General's investigation of ticket distribution practices is notable for the number of anonymous letters and phone calls it has given rise to and the number of industry insiders who express consternation at the current system of ticket distribution, but who will not speak for attribution. The Attorney General has concluded that the practice of paying and receiving ice is rampant;(33) that creators and producers are tired of it because they believe the excess money in the system rightfully should be theirs(34) and reports in the press repeatedly carry unsourced quotes acknowledging the existence of ice and its "inevitability."

There is little movement in or out of the career of ticket selling, except that some ticket sellers become ticket brokers. While ticket sellers do not seem to change careers, they frequently move from box office to box office, primarily within the same organization, e.g., the Shubert or the Nederlander chain, but also between organizations.(35) Box office treasurers and ticket sellers are generally part of a tightly knit group that includes fathers, sons, brothers, in-laws and many other familial relationships.

Original sellers of tickets and ticket resellers have closed ranks because the substantial livelihood of both groups is at stake. One New Jersey ticket reseller, the owner of a New Jersey ticket brokerage business, came to the attention of the Attorney General through records showing that he and his employees purchased 700 tickets to *The Lion King* at the box office during ten days in July, 1997. (See Exhibit L, consisting of 23 pages of copies of credit card receipts in the name of the owner of the ticket brokerage firm, Ticket Town, and a cover page summarizing his purchases by date and time of day). On July 26, 1997, 164 such purchases were executed in 29 minutes and on July 28, 1998, 230 transactions took place in 40 minutes. Yet, the head of the New Amsterdam Theatre box office claimed he was not familiar with the purchaser. Testifying under oath at a hearing conducted by the Attorney General, the manager of the New Amsterdam

Theatre box office (where *The Lion King* opened on November 13, 1997, after enormous advance publicity), stated that he did not know the purchaser, but remembered that his staff complained about processing his orders. The ticket broker refused to testify and only did so after he was granted immunity and faced being arrested on criminal contempt charges. Claiming to specialize in Broadway show ticket resale, he maintained in his July 28, 1998 testimony that he particularly specialized in only two shows, *The Lion King* and *Chicago*. Despite having a business with four full-time employees and drawing a salary of approximately $125,000 per year, he was unable to give even the most rudimentary information about his business, such as his yearly gross, how many tickets he sells in an average week or even how many tickets were sold the day before his testimony. He willingly attested to his own illegal conduct of reselling $75 Broadway show tickets for anywhere between two and three times their face value, conduct for which he could not be prosecuted pursuant to his immunity agreement. He did not, however, advance the investigation with respect to sources or payments of ice.

Other corroborative evidence has been collected during the investigation. For instance, Exhibit M, is a list of telephone calls made in 1996 to illegal ticket brokers from the Broadway box offices of the theatres showing the four most popular shows on Broadway, *The Phantom of the Opera*, *Les Miserables*, *Miss Saigon* and *Chicago*. Similarly, Exhibit N is a proposal for "de-bugging" the home of a former box office supervisor at MSG sent to V.I.P. Tickets, an unlicensed New York ticket broker.

D. Agents of the Venue: Ticketmaster and Telecharge

Ticketmaster dominates the field of providing computerized ticket services to venues. It is the ticketing agent for almost every major concert and sports venue in New York, as well as for the Nederlander chain of theatres, Disney's New Amsterdam Theatre (where *The Lion King* is playing) and the Ford Center for the Performing Arts (currently showing *Ragtime*). The only competition Ticketmaster now faces in New York is Telecharge, developed and owned by the Shubert Organization, the owner of 16 Broadway theatres. Telecharge handles the telephone call-in operations for Shubert Theatres, as well as for the Jujamcyn Theatres, the owners of five theatres, and the National Tennis Center. Unlike Ticketmaster, Telecharge does not have remote walk-in outlets.

The standard Ticketmaster arrangement with a venue is to provide all ticket selling services for an event,(36) including accounting and inventory control. Regardless of where the tickets are sold— at the box office, through a centralized telephone system or at a walk-in-Ticketmaster outlet or elsewhere—the tickets will be issued from a Ticketmaster terminal.(37) All terminals have access to the same supply of tickets—those that the venue has agreed to sell to the public. At the commencement of sale the computer terminals cannot access tickets that have previously been placed in a "hold" status. Generally, unless a certain number of seats have been expressly held for sale at the box office, the terminals in the box office have no advantage over those in telephone rooms or outlets—it is first come, first serve, no matter which terminal sends the order.

Ticketmaster's remote outlets—approximately 120 throughout the tri-state area of New York, New Jersey and Connecticut— are, however, in terms of control and accountability, the weakest link in the system. The people who operate outlet terminals are either minimum-wage hourly workers at such chains as HMV or Rite Aid drug stores(38) or small entrepeneurships, such as sneaker stores and frequently, video stores.(39) In either case, there is almost no accountability for the terminal operators. There are consistent reports from informants in the ticket resale business about how certain small outlets have links with certain ticket brokers; that certain ticket brokers even control groups of Ticketmaster outlets. Indeed, the Attorney General's Office has obtained evidence that a particular video store and Ticketmaster outlet located in the Bronx is silently owned by a New Jersey ticket broker. Ticketmaster management has worked cooperatively with the Attorney General, including forwarding a communication it received from an independent outlet describing a person who offered to pay "thousands of dollars for preferential treatment during on-sales." See Exhibit O.

The methods used at such outlets to divert tickets to brokers are relatively simple. A terminal operator at an outlet may issue tickets for a minute or two prior to admitting the first public customer or in between customers, to convey tickets to an illegal reseller. The price of the ticket plus any legitimate service fee is paid. As in all such illicit ticket transactions, the venue is always made whole. The ice is paid to the terminal operator in cash by the ticket broker. Based on numerous reports of such activities, the Attorney General commenced an inquiry by examining the printouts of Ticketmaster outlets subsequent to the sale of tickets to the 1994 Barbra Streisand concerts at Madison Square Garden. Testimony on the findings of that inquiry was presented to the New York Assembly Committee on Tourism, Arts and Sports Development.(40)

Among the observations resulting from the Attorney General's inquiry were: (1) certain outlets had a higher number of transactions per unit of time than others (i.e., the time between transactions was only fifteen to twenty seconds as opposed to one to two minutes); and (2) all tickets were sold only in certain multiples, such as blocks of four or blocks of six, whereas it would have been unlikely for all fans on line to have wanted or needed the same number of tickets. Based on these other selling patterns, certain outlets were targeted for further inquiry.

The Attorney General found that 70 percent of the tickets issued at targeted outlets found their way into the resale market. The printout of one closely investigated Long Island outlet was totally irreconcilable with what was observed at that outlet. According to the printout, there were 40 transactions during a time frame when only 17 people were observed to have purchased tickets. Furthermore, the first person from the line to make a purchase actually obtained the sixth set of tickets issued, the sixth person obtained the 22nd and so forth, leading to the conclusion that the outlet operator was setting aside or purchasing tickets, in between sales, for resale to a ticket broker for personal profit. Interviews conducted at Madison Square Garden of persons sitting in the particular seats sold at that outlet confirmed that the tickets represented by the 23 transactions occurring when no one was on the line were resold by a Connecticut ticket broker. Fans who called the Attorney General's Office provided ample support for the conclusion that similar scenarios occur at other outlets in connection with other concerts. One caller who stood on line at a Tower Records outlet for Backstreet Boys tickets on March 21, 1998, said that the tickets were sold out before the doors even opened.

In connection with the sale of tickets to the 1998 Spice Girls concerts at Madison Square Garden, the Daily News reported:

[I]t appears merchants or their employees sold four-ticket blocks faster than humanly possible—an indication that they were siphoning off tickets for themselves, friends or scalpers.

In the most glaring example, 72 tickets were sold at one Manhattan outlet in the first three minutes. That translates to 18 sales of four-tickets blocks—impossible, given the time required to print the tickets after taking each customer's order.

Ticketmaster has acknowledged that it may have had a problem at some outlets, particularly, small, independent outlets at such places as video stores and sneaker stores, but that it has taken necessary corrective actions. Ticketmaster also points to the difficulties it has encountered in attempts to terminate contracts of certain outlets for engaging in preferential and improper sales. Indeed, Ticketmaster's standard form contract with its outlets contains the following language:

[name of outlet] may only sell Tickets to customers physically present at a location. [name of outlet] may not accept orders for tickets or effect sales of Tickets by telephone.

*   *   *

Scalping or brokering of Tickets by [name of outlet] or any employee or agent of [name of outlet], or the providing of Tickets to third party scalpers or brokers through preferential sale or otherwise, or the providing of inside information concerning Attractions, will be considered to be a material breach of this Agreement and, in the event of such activity, Ticketmaster may terminate this Agreement immediately.

Nevertheless, Ticketmaster's attempt to terminate its contract with a video store, Night at the Movies, Inc. ("NATM") for breach of contract, resulted in extended litigation. Court papers submitted by Ticketmaster describe its investigation of NATM. A Ticketmaster employee was sent to monitor NATM on November 14, 1997. A new block of *The Lion King* tickets were to go on sale that morning. The employee/monitor arrived at NATM prior to 8 a.m. The store's security gate was half-closed and its door was apparently locked. He never lost sight of the store entrance between approximately 7:55 a.m. and 8:10 a.m. when he knocked on the still-locked door. There were no customers in the store during that 15 minute period, yet the computer printout showed that between 8:00 a.m. and 8:05 a.m., 18 "Lion King" tickets were pulled for cash transactions at precisely 8:00 a.m., six more at 8:01 a.m. and an additional five were pulled at 8:03, all charged to someone said by NATM to be a bona fide customer. Since no one was in the store at the time, however, it is likely that a NATM employee simply used that credit card to cover illicit transactions.

The above-related incident indicates the number of ways that tickets can be diverted from the primary market to the illegal resale market in the span of three minutes. First, information that a new block of *The Lion King* tickets was going on sale was closely held; second, Ticketmaster outlet employees were pulling tickets for themselves; and third, surrogate credit card numbers were used as a cover for the purchase of tickets by insiders without the credit card holder having been present at the outlet.(41)

Ticketmaster appears to be attempting to phase out independent outlets and claims that all outlet sales account for only about 30 percent of its sales in the Northeast region. Some of the more recently opened outlets like The Wiz are staffed by hourly employees whose duties extend beyond ticket sales. There is, therefore, even less supervision and regulation of Ticketmaster outlets than there is of box offices.

E. The Use of Diggers: The Myth and the Reality

It is a myth that homeless persons account for the supply of tickets in the resale market. While many individuals are paid to stand on ticket lines, this does not account for the huge supply of tickets—certainly not for the huge supply of the best tickets—in the secondary market.

To the contrary, the primary manner tickets are diverted to the resale market is by employees of venues, as well as promoters and other insiders. Indeed, if homeless people simply stood on line like the rest of us, their chances of obtaining tickets to a "hot" event would be equal to those of the rest of us. They would have no better chance than anyone else on the line of getting the front row center, or whatever is the most desirable seat. But these are exactly the seats that unlicensed brokers have, and in large quantity, to supply their corporate customers who are willing to pay premium prices for such seats. Having the best seats is exactly what these brokers advertise.

To be sure, the use of "diggers" is one method ticket brokers/scalpers use to monopolize the supply of tickets to particular events. Brokers even have their own groups of diggers or "crews." Large brokers may have as many as 100 to 200 diggers in their crew.

This has undoubtedly led to the numerous complainants who have described the chaotic and intimidating scene at a venue when diggers arrive. They have no trouble identifying diggers, although security details retained by the venue are supposedly unable to make such observations, according to their testimony. Often the diggers engage in intimidation, literally taking any place in line they choose with apparent impunity.

The following letter received by the Attorney General's Office regarding a digger infested ticket sale at Radio City Music Hall for "Radiohead" (1998 Grammy winner for best alternative

performance) typifies the many other such complaints this office
has received:

Tickets "originally" were to go on sale . . . Saturday March 7th
[1998] through Ticketmaster and the Radio City Music Hall
box office. As a Radiohead fan, I had heard a rumor that wrist
bands (for a place on line to buy tickets at the box office the next
day) for the up coming concerts were going to be distributed at a
side door of Radio City, between 5:00 and 9:00 p.m. on Friday
March 6th. I arrived at the side door located in the middle of
51st street between 5th and 6th Avenues, at 5:00 p.m. where I
found around 25 people waiting on an orderly line.

For two hours I waited with my friend, his mother and girl-
friend and my wife as the line grew longer. About 7:00 p.m.
groups of people began to arrive, most of which arrived by several cars and vans and simpl[y] proceeded to push and intimidate
their way to the front of the line having no regard for anyone
that had been waiting in line. By 8:00 p.m. the line had grown
to roughly 300 rowdy people with the majority at the front,
pushing towards the door. Without passing judgement, and trying to be as charitable as possible, [I] . . . . feel I can safely say
that at least 80% of the people on the line had no idea what artist
was playing in the concert they were waiting for, let alone considered themselves a fan of the artist. These people were clearly
part of [a] well-organized system for scalpers to obtain the best
tickets for illegal resale of the tickets at inflated prices.

I should also add that there was clearly inadequate security to
control the mass of people. The only security officer we ha[d]
seen was the one who told us not to sit on the street around 5:00
p.m. when there was still only 25 people on line. After my wife
told me that she had witnessed several drug deals, and fearing for

the safety of the women, my friend and I advised them to wait in the TV Land restaurant on the corner. The girl in front of us who had been there when I arrived, probably no older than 23 and less than 5 feet tall, was so intimidated by the arriving hoards that she fled after already waiting for almost three hours. After great stress and danger, my friend and I finally got our wrist bands by 8:00 p.m. Words can't truly explain how happy I was to be free of that situation. That night I could not fall asleep until 4:30 in the morning because my heart was still racing at the insensitivity, intimidation and lack of security that I had witnessed that evening outside of Radio City Music Hall.

To give Radio City their credit, when I went down on Saturday morning to buy tickets, there were numerous staff/security people that made sure everyone was in numerical order, according to the number on their randomly selected wrist band. My question, along with all the other fans I spoke with, was, where were the security personnel the previous night when no sense or order was maintained?

It would be obvious to anyone that these people were scalpers looking to make a fast buck at the expense of the New York City, Radio City Music Hall and especially the fans, without whom the concert could not be held. I should also note that the pamphlet distributed with the wrist band entitled "Ticket Sales Information" specifically states the following, that any rational man or women would say were violated that evening. I will enclose a copy of the entire pamphlet for your benefit. I quote:

1) Any person observed disrupting or breaking the line will not be permitted to receive a wrist band or to purchase tickets.

2) Anyone reselling tickets, or attempting to purchase tickets with the intent to resell them, will be denied the right to participate in the wrist banding process or to buy tickets.

I understand the demand for an event like this outstrips the supply: it is the nature of show business. But that does not mean the safety and well being of . . . New York's citizens should be in jeopardy, nor should Radio City Music Hall, the City of New York or the Artists in the concert lose out on money that is going in the pockets of scalpers. Radio City Music Hall is a treasured and culturally significant part of New York City and it belittles the integrity of the institution and the city to allow tickets to be distributed in this manner.

The testimony of persons who have stood on ticket lines with diggers and engaged them in conversation is that they are recruited at places such as the Port Authority bus terminal to stand on line to purchase tickets or obtain numbered wrist bands for major concerts. They are recruited on behalf of ticket brokers by a person known as a "crew boss" who is usually visibly stationed near the scene of an on-sale with the cash for the purchase of tickets and to pay the diggers their fee—which is said to go as high as $60.

One mother of a young Spice Girls fan gave the Attorney General's Office a virtual reality tour of the atmosphere outside Madison Square Garden the night before Spice Girls tickets for their July, 1998 concerts were put on sale. Her account is set forth in great detail to give the reader a sense of the scene. She arrived with her beach chair at 10:00 p.m. the evening before the on-sale with eight friends. At that time, she estimated there were about 50 people ahead of her. At midnight, when numbered wrist bands were distributed, the orderly line of fans was overrun by approximately 100 diggers. The wrist bands were blue or green and pink. Diggers had blue or green wrist bands. The fans wound up with the pink. Continuing her story, the witness said she started talking to a digger whom she identified by name. He told her he was from Levittown and was currently collecting welfare. She gave him money to buy coffee. He told her that anyone with a pink wrist band, such as she had, would not get to purchase tickets. As the night wore on she decided to offer him $150 to purchase tickets for her instead of the crew boss from whom he would get only $50. He checked with his crew boss, who apparently agreed to let him make the extra money. At approximately 7:00 a.m. people with blue wrist bands were let into the building. Shortly thereafter it was announced that only 800 tickets were being sold at that location and, as the digger had predicted hours earlier, all persons with pink wrist bands could leave. The digger enlisted a friend to fulfill his agreement to purchase tickets for the complainant. The friend came out at between 9:05 and 9:10 a.m. with four tickets in the uppermost row of seats.

The foregoing account of the digger activity on this night is corroborated by ticket terminal records showing numerous consecutive cash transactions for the maximum number of tickets permitted to be purchased in one transaction. On this basis, it appears that 37 diggers purchased the first 148 tickets sold. All of these seats were among the "best" seats sold for the concert and the best seats sold at the box office. Madison Square Garden security personnel, however, including the two persons who were in charge of security on the morning of the on-sale and the night before, testified that they were unaware of any digger activity. In response to a specific question about diggers, the Supervisor of Events Operations stated: "No, no, I don't know who they are."

While diggers are perhaps the most visible part of the underground economy that supports the ticket resale market and probably the most irritating to fans, to a certain extent diggers actually camouflage the more insidious corruption of the ticket distribution system.

F. Mail Orders

During an on-site visit by the Attorney General's staff, a knowledgeable theatre executive divulged what he called a well-kept secret—that the best way for the public to assure itself of obtaining good seats to a new show is by mail order, since mail orders are filled prior to phone and walk-in orders. This well-kept secret is, however, an open secret to ticket brokers who exploit this method extensively by using the individual names and addresses of their employees and other associates to obtain excellent seats before they are made available to the public. The use of mail orders by brokers appears to be part of an elaborate scheme between the brokers and individuals at the venues to cover up the fact that the brokers are draining highly desirable seats prior to the general sale to the public. A review of letters accompanying mail orders to a number of Broadway shows has shown letters with a surface similarity—all seeking the same number of tickets—are in fact from the employees of one ticket broker, Red Mark Entertainment. See Exhibit P. Although only one of these letters requests Saturday evening tickets, all of the orders were filled with top quality Saturday evening tickets. An additional 7 letters were notable because: (1) three were almost identical letters (two signed by the same person) requesting tickets for different dates, but identical seat locations; (2) the telephone numbers on three letters are the same; and (3) in some instances letters to certain venues provide unnecessary details e.g., "my family is coming in from California for a visit and this will be a surprise for them" as if to provide a cover of legitimacy for the order. See Exhibit Q. Most notably, when the addresses on a number of such letters were visited by the Attorney General's investigators, they were, in fact, not residences, but ticket brokers in Fort Lee and Union City, New Jersey.

IV. SEATS THAT ARE NEVER AVAILABLE TO THE GENERAL PUBLIC

The chief obstacle to equal access and lower prices is the illicit and lawful diversion of tickets from the general public. There is a finite number of tickets available for any event, but in too many cases particularly the most coveted events, as many as 90% of the tickets are diverted from the general public. Diversion occurs both illicitly and lawfully, albeit unfairly.
Report to New Jersey Governor
Christine Todd Whitman
On Access to Entertainment in New Jersey

"House seats" or "house pulls" or "management pulls" or "producer pulls" or "promoter pulls" are the "coin of the realm" in the entertainment and sports industry and in the more extensive business community. Simply put, access to house seats represents power. High quality seats are beyond the average consumer's reach. Indeed, the number of seats withheld from public sale for all major events seems to have increased continuously in recent years so that the most desirable seats simply are not available to the fan who lacks either the connections or the assets necessary to purchase tickets from illegal brokers. Even the fan who stands on line all night and is the first at the ticket window will not be able to get tickets near the stage or playing field. In addition to traditional house seat holders—such as persons associated with a production or sports events (e.g., athletes, performers, creators, producers, promoters, owners, or agents)—consignees such as credit card companies capture increasing quantities of the most desirable tickets and use them for marketing purposes.

A. Theatre Parties and Group Sales

Before opening, shows are extensively marketed to theatre party sales agents and subsequently to group sales agents who may purchase anywhere from 20 tickets to the entire house for a particular performance. These agents, in turn, engage in extensive marketing to groups such as charitable organizations—which are exempt from the maximum premium price provision of the law—and other groups. Group sales agents do not screen their clients as to whether they are legitimate organizations. Exhibit R sets forth a list of clients of the theatre party and group sales agents who sold tickets for *The Lion King* performances during the three-month period from November 15, 1997 to February 15, 1998, the date of each performance and the number of tickets purchased

If the theatre party is a large one, the performance is denominated a "party pull", which means that certain house seats become part of the theatre party seats and are not available to the house seat holder. On such occasions, however, although a certain number of seats are reserved for the theatre party, some unused house seats may be returned to the venue. Whether there are unused house seats for a party pull performance may be learned at any time until eight weeks prior to the performance, when the final payment from the group sales agent is due. At this time, these unused house seats are supposed to go into open inventory, but frequently wind up in the hands of illegal ticket brokers.

Of course, a group sales agent may order more tickets than are actually purchased by a particular group and sell those tickets to a ticket broker or simply place a group order for a ticket broker. See Exhibit S. These practices would be in violation of the contract such agents have with the theatres, but the theatres consistently state that they have no way to police the sales agents.

B. Manipulation of House Seats

The manipulation of the house seat system appears to be a primary way that desirable tickets reach the hands of illegal brokers. Some house seats are sold on a retail basis by persons (such as performers and creators) who are contractually entitled to seats for each performance of a Broadway play, and who provide them to a ticket broker for a premium as part of an ongoing arrangement. This, however, represents only a small number of tickets. At the other end of the spectrum, hundreds of tickets can be made available to illegal ticket brokers from the multitude of tickets withheld from public sale for a long list of parties related to certain events. For a typical concert, tickets are held for the act, the promoter, the talent agency, the record company, corporate sponsors, advertisers, marketing and promotional campaigns, "give aways," corporate suite holders and, of course, the "house." Some typical lists of holds are attached as Exhibit T. These tickets are also referred to as being "on consignment," meaning that they are held until purchased or, at a certain time, returned to inventory. Reserved seats must be paid for at the time they are actually taken by the consignee (except for relatively few complementary tickets or "comps"). If the tickets are not picked up, they are supposed to be returned to inventory for sale to the general public.

1. Theatre House Seats

House seats are generally handled on a designated house seat telephone line by a house seat operator (not necessarily located in the box office) who takes the order, writes up a house seat order form and conveys it to the box office where a house seat holder or a designee can pick up the tickets. If a house seat is not purchased by 48 hours (generally) prior to the performance, it is "released"—no longer kept in a hold status—and becomes available for sale.

During the weeks after the opening of a hit show, persons entitled to the use of the seats and their friends and relatives may use the seats. Into the run of the show, the demand by authorized house seats holders inevitably decreases. Experienced box office employees have become familiar with this pattern and sell these seats directly to brokers either at the time (generally 48 hours before the show) when they are supposed to go back into the system for sale to the general public, or even before such time, as the Attorney General's investigation has established. Exhibit U—compiled by the Attorney General's Office from records of ticket sales for the period April through July 1994 for *Beauty and the Beast* and *Grease*—shows the actual dates of sale of house seats and the dates of the performances. All of these sales to illegal brokers (those who generally resell at mark-ups of over 100 percent) took place during the time such seats were supposedly being held for house seat holders and therefore were not available for sale to the general public. Exhibit V, also compiled from records of ticket sales for *Beauty and the Beast* for the period of April through July 1994, shows that even those house seats that were held until the scheduled release were sold to ticket brokers and not returned to inventory for sale to the general public. This compilation shows almost 1000 house seats—some that were to be held for emergencies, others that were part of a "party pull"—all of which were sold to illegal brokers within the 24-hour period prior to the performance when they should have been available to the public.

Isolated seats placed in a hold status may never be detected. Thus, for example, certain seats may be sold to a ticket broker for every performance of a Broadway show. A supervisor, assuming that they are house seats because of their desirable location, may never become aware of it. This is what happened at the Virginia Theatre for a period of approximately 14 months during the run of *Smokey Joe's Cafe*. The treasurer and assistant treasurer were ultimately fired by Jujamcyn Theatre for their activities, which consisted of "unauthorized statusing" (placing certain seats in a computer hold status that blocked their sale to the general public) of more than 500 seats. Because the locations so status-ed were premium orchestra seats (C109-114), management simply assumed they were house seats off sale to the general public.

2. Concert Holds

All unused concert holds are supposed to be returned to inventory for sale to the public. That is why sometimes a block of tickets may become available even on the day of the performance. Such tickets, however, generally also do not become available to the public. For the July 1, 1998 Spice Girls concert at Madison Square Garden there were to be 4,583 holds, according to the venue. See Exhibit T. In fact, according to subsequent records, SFX, the owner of promoter Delsener/Slater Enterprises ("Delsener/Slater") obtained an additional 217 tickets over its originally stated allotment of 200 tickets; Delsener/Slater likewise received an additional 78 tickets; and MSG management received an additional 72 tickets. For its Spice Girls analysis, the Attorney General's Office defined 4,750 seats as "best seats." Of these, only 1,154 were available for public sale, at least 148 of which were sold to diggers. The remaining 3,442 were held for various purposes, including 378 for the promoter.

Interviews conducted by the Attorney General's staff on the night of the Spice Girls concert with persons sitting in seats withheld from public sale establish that such seats were sold by illegal ticket brokers. Twenty-four people sitting in floor seats withheld for Delsener/Slater acknowledged that their tickets were purchased from ticket brokers. Two of these tickets were purchased from Taramack Tickets in Westchester, against which the Attorney

General commenced a civil action, obtaining a default order and judgement.

Manipulation of the hold system occurs in various ways. In addition to grossly understating the number of tickets to be withheld from public sale, venue personnel appear to take earmarked for sale to the public out of the system just prior to the public sale. The Attorney General has examined the records of sales for six 1998 concerts at MSG—the Spice Girls on July 1, 1998, Celine Dion on September 3-4, 1998, and three Eric Clapton concerts on April 18-20, 1998. For these six concerts, 452 seats—originally designated for public sale—were not sold to the public on the on-sale days, but were held in a management hold status and subsequently sold at the box office by the current manager of box office operations and other ticket sellers. See Exhibit W. Similarly, for the July 17, 1998 Back Street Boys concert at Radio City Music Hall ("RCMH") 159 tickets were placed into a hold status, although no such status was designated on RCMH's manifest for that concert. See Exhibit X. These tickets were sold for cash after the March 21, 1998 public sale. See Exhibit Y.

The fraudulent scheme that occurred at the Jones Beach Marine Theater in 1996 was also based on the illicit placing of tickets into a hold status by the box office treasurer and assistant treasurer. As a result of scrutiny by the management of the band Hootie and the Blowfish, it became evident that tickets in the first ten rows for 37 of the concerts that summer were withheld from public sale (tickets for all concerts went on sale on the same day) and were subsequently sold to ticket brokers. The tickets withheld were valued at $300,000. Head treasurer Joseph Nekola ultimately pled guilty to grand larceny in the second degree, a Class C felony, and computer tampering in the third degree, a Class E felony.

3. Ticket Clubs

There are two major concert promoters in the New York area, Delsener/Slater and Metropolitan Entertainment ("Metropolitan"). Delsener/Slater, acquired in recent years by SFX, is by far the larger. Both organizations maintain their own "ticket clubs" of fee-paying members. In 1994, Metropolitan's club had between 100 and 200 members (which it still has); Delsener/Slater's club had 400 members.

The concert promoter controls the original allocation of tickets to a concert. The number of tickets to which the promoter is entitled (a certain number are generally complimentary; the others are required to be paid for) is controlled by the promoter's contract with the venue. These tickets are, of course, among the best.

Before Delsener/Slater changed its policy and created its tiered membership system during 1997-98 and targeted corporate clients, its club members were offered a maximum of two tickets per concert, as were Metropolitan's members. On the basis of the above numbers, the maximum number of tickets that could possibly have been allocated to members for one concert was 800 for Delsener/Slater club members and 400 for Metropolitan club members. In fact, for the series of Barbra Streisand concerts at MSG in 1994, Delsener/Slater allocated 2400 tickets for itself, 1600 tickets more than required for club members, even assuming that every club member chose to attend a Streisand concert. MSG records for the September 4, 1998 Celine Dion concert show a similar pattern. For that concert Metropolitan allocated 1769 tickets for itself, 1369 tickets more than were required for Metropolitan's club membership. At least 14 of these tickets were offered for sale by Maxx Entertainment, Inc., a Connecticut ticket broker.

The new Delsener/Slater ticket club structure created tiered memberships, aimed at attracting corporate clients, for fees ranging from $250 to $5000. Information on the exact number of Delsener/Slater club members is not available at the time of this writing. However, if the above described pattern still holds, it appears that both Delsener/Slater and Metropolitan take substantially more tickets for each concert than warranted by the number of club members. Many tickets allocated to both promoters ultimately wind up in the hands of illegal ticket resellers.

The total income that can be derived from a ticket club based on the number of ticket club members, their membership and service fees—an estimated $70,000 for Metropolitan in 1998, before costs—does not appear to provide a sufficient financial incentive for organizing a ticket club. Accordingly, the inference that clubs serve as a vehicle for a lucrative trade with ticket brokers appears inescapable.

4. Sporting Events: The Subscription List

Most Knicks and Rangers subscriptions are sold to persons who have connections with the management of MSG. These persons include personal and professional acquaintances, business affiliates, as well as many celebrities. Indeed, 75 percent of the Knicks season subscriptions that became available in 1997 were management connected. The 25 per cent that were sold to the public were all located in the upper tier.

Ticket brokers or persons who obtain tickets for ticket brokers also obtain subscriptions through management. For example, Patrick J. Lynch, the owner of Curtain Call, a New Jersey ticket brokerage firm was on the management list with the notation that he was involved with MSG boxing, casting considerable doubt on the validity of the information on that list. Lynch obtained a subscription in 1997, more than a year after an internal MSG investigation (which resulted in the termination of five employees in its subscription department). As a result of that investigation, the three Knicks subscriptions and one Ranger subscription of the owner and employees of a New Jersey ticket brokerage, Prime Entertainment, were canceled. Despite the 1996 cancellation, Prime Entertainment obtained four Knicks subscriptions and one Rangers subscription in 1997, which were sold to its owner Gary Basse and three employees. Gary Shapiro of Great Seats, whose subscription was also canceled in 1996, reappeared on the 1997 subscription list. Scott Gould, who already had multiple Knicks and Rangers subscriptions, was on the 1996 list as requesting additional subscriptions. Despite MSG's express policy that subscribers who resell tickets forfeit their subscription rights, he sold tickets to Ticket Window, which is also known as 1-800 TICKETS.

In addition, eight other Knicks and six other Rangers subscribers who had subscriptions canceled in 1996 reappeared as subscribers in 1997. Indeed, 71 Knicks and 47 Rangers subscriptions were still being held by resellers after the internal investigation. Exhibits Z and AA. A holder of one of these subscriptions, the Nederlander Organization, sells seats to the ticket broker Redmark through Scott Nederlander. Exhibit BB. Another one of these resellers is a member of MSG's security staff who holds four Knicks subscriptions in total, three of these in association with his accountant. Individual tickets that were part of these subscriptions were sold by an illegal ticket broker—Your Ticket Place. This accountant testified before the Attorney General that he owns 12 Rangers and 12 Knicks seasons subscriptions. Ten of these subscriptions were obtained through a vice president of finance and a seasons subscriptions employee. This employee also provides the accountant with tickets to concerts, and is the same person who made the above mentioned arrangements for both Patrick Lynch and Scott Gould.

The accountant also testified that he generally gave these tickets to clients and employees or sold them at face price. In addition, he testified that he exchanged his seats with theatre connected people for Broadway shows and with out-of-state ticket brokers. He also sold some to ticket brokers. Indeed, some of these seats were resold by Your Ticket Place and Concert Connection, Connecticut ticket brokers.

V. INDUSTRY SELF-POLICING

The stance of the venues, as well as Ticketmaster and Telecharge (original ticket distributors), has been cooperative throughout this investigation. Substantial information has been provided to the Attorney General's Office voluntarily or pursuant to subpoena. It appears that as a result of the Attorney General's request for or subpoena of information and subsequent discussions of problem areas, or independently, some of the original ticket distributors have undertaken to institute reforms. However, even the positive steps they have taken to clear up the ticket distribution process have been reactive rather than proactive. The evidence of fraudulent or illegal conduct by individual or groups of employees at venues or in the employ of Ticketmaster is there to be seen by those employers. Some examples of measures taken by venues in reaction to the Attorney General's investigation and, in some instances, the concomitant press attention are:

In 1996, MSG terminated, for cause, five employees who worked in their box office and season subscription department, subsequent to an internal investigation that received assistance from the Attorney General's Office.

It was discovered at a Jujamcyn theatre that its treasurer and an assistant treasurer were placing a block of six tickets in hold status for every performance of a show without the authorization or knowledge of management. When this was discovered, approximately 18 months into the show, the employees were terminated. They were, however, subsequently hired by other venues—one by the Nederlander Organization, the other by Radio City Music Hall.

As a result of an internal investigation of the practices of its box office employees, in May 1996, "RCMH" took advantage of a provision of its contract with Local 751 of the Treasurers and Ticket sellers union, which permitted it to issue a non-renewal notice to its members once a year, without cause, during a 30-day period at the expiration of the contract period. RCMH purchased tickets to many of its own concerts from illegal brokers (to wit: Global Travel and Entertainment Inc., Liberty Theatre Ticket Service and Turf Tickets) and was able to trace them back to individual ticket sellers in the box office. They placed these people under surveillance and established that one of them was having regular meetings in a nearby restaurant with a former RCMH box office employee who was now a ticket broker. Other individuals under surveillance appeared to have different contacts. RCMH decided to take advantage of the above contract provision and therefore terminated the employment of its box office staff and one supervisor, but not the head treasurer, and hired new personnel as of June 1, 1996. Many of the terminated employees, however, are now simply working at other venues.

In a change of policy in February, 1998, the New Amsterdam Theatre reduced the number of tickets that could be purchased in one transaction by telephone or at an outlet from 19 to two. Prior to this time, documents obtained by the Attorney General showed illegal brokers and their associates obtaining hundreds of *The Lion King* tickets by this method. See Section III, A.

After an outpouring of complaints about diggers obtaining all of the wrist-bands and buying up all of the tickets available for sale at the box office on April 17, 1998 for the July 1, 1998 Spice Girls concert, MSG announced that its box office would no longer be open for first-day sales, i.e., tickets could only be purchased by telephone or at Ticketmaster outlets.

Some venues, such as Disney's New Amsterdam Theatre have taken steps to decrease the number of house seats withheld from public sale, although theatres generally decrease the number of house seats during the run of a show, in any event, as the demand for them decreases. The Attorney General is asking the theatre community to participate in a voluntary, concerted effort to cut down on the number of house seats from the inception of a show.

VI. POLICY AND LEGISLATIVE ISSUES

A. Policy

1. Perception of Unfairness

It's not murder or drug-running. No one is really hurt. Some people may not get into a concert or sporting event or they may get the worst seats in the house, even though they have waited on line for hours or they may resort to scalpers and illegal ticket brokers. Theatre goers, the industry repeatedly avers, do not suffer harm because tickets are available for the duration of the run of a play which can be for many years depending upon its continued popularity with the public. Gerald Schoenfeld, Chairman of the Shubert Organization, Inc. testifying in this regard, stated:

[D]espite suggestions to the contrary, someone who is willing to wait for a desired seat location will be able to purchase such a seat. If a specific desired location is not available at a particular time, that seat, or one nearby, will be available at a later date.

The "victimless crime" or "what's the harm" argument ignores the fact that a system perceived as both unfair and corrupt ultimately injures the industry that supports it. Recent reports have focused on the fact that the audience for the legitimate theatre is growing older and for the most part is not being replaced by younger audiences. Although several initiatives have been undertaken to attract young people to the theatre, even some creating a limited number of low cost tickets, none have addressed the perception of systemic unfairness in the ticket distribution system, which renders unavailable good seats to popular shows at inflated prices in a reasonable amount of time.

Illegal ticket resellers are able to provide (even guarantee) the best seats to the most popular shows within a matter of a day or two. They are even willing to sell (to take orders for) tickets that have not gone on sale yet. They know with certainty that they will have certain seats. This puts the lie to the claim that they are standing on line or calling just like anyone else (an act which in and of itself would not be illegal). Clearly, their business depends on pre-arrangements with insiders who control the vast percentage of best seats.

An investigator on the Attorney General's staff was able to obtain guarantees for Saturday night seats, in the first 15 rows (or the first five rows in the mezzanine), "prime seats" as they were described by the order taker, for several popular Broadway musicals within a week's time. The investigator was advised, however, that the tickets could not be mailed to him. The explanation was as follows:

Usually that's not possible for Broadway shows, although our agent [the speaker was an employee of American Express—their "agent" in this exchange is the ticket broker] can confirm tickets, they, you know, yes, one hundred percent, I guarantee I can provide these tickets. They don't actually, the tickets aren't unavailable [sic] to them until like the day before, sometimes the day of the show. So usually for Broadway shows we have to arrange to have them left at the box office. Very rarely do agents actually have them in hand in enough time to even have them Federal Expressed out. This is something that we do all the time. Again, I've never had a problem with having tickets left at the box office either.

It could be concluded from this exchange that the tickets were not actually available at that time because they were unreleased house seats required to be held until 48 hours before the performance, and that there was an arrangement that when the seats were released they would be sold to the broker rather than sold to the public. See Discussion of House Seats supra and Exhibits U and V.

2. Tax Consequences

One consequence of the underground economy in tickets is the loss of income tax revenues to the State of New York, as well as the City of New York and the federal government, resulting from illegal, unreported cash payments of ice to box office employees and other insiders.

In addition, illegal ticket resellers pay no sales tax on the huge mark-ups for which tickets sell on the resale market, sometimes rising to thousands of dollars for such events as the Knicks playoffs or the series of Barbra Streisand concerts in 1994. In a case brought by the Attorney General's Office against an unlicensed New York ticket reseller, a trial jury found the co-owners of Tickets on Request guilty of both reselling tickets for over the maximum premium price and of tax evasion by failing to collect $35,000 in sales taxes.

However, the trial court set aside the verdict on the tax charges. The Court found that while sales tax is required to be collected upon an admission charge, this requirement is not applicable to a service fee imposed by a subsequent seller, since this service charge is essentially unrelated to the price of admission. The Court considered the fact that state legislation had been recently introduced which would have amended the definition of "admission charge" in the Tax Law to include the mark-ups charged by brokers such as the defendants. Since this amendment had not yet been enacted, the Court concluded "that the legislative view is clearly that such tax obligations do not exist under current law."

3. Profits Derived from the Sale of Tickets Rightfully Inure to Investors and Creators

Nothing but an apparently self-imposed stricture and concern about the public perception prevents theatres, sport and concert venues, the source of the original sale of a ticket, to establish any price the market will allow on its tickets. There has been much recent talk about the so-called "free market." The market is indeed free at the point where the original sale price of a ticket is set, at the place of entertainment. These original issuers theoretically lose huge amounts of money by allowing their agents and employees who receive ice and the illegal ticket brokers who pay it to take in the difference between the established price of tickets and the amount they actually command in the marketplace.

If there is excess demand in the system which results in excess profits, these profits should not, in fairness, become a windfall for people who add no value to the product represented by the ticket. The people who should be participating in such gains are the creative people who produce the product and the investors or risk takers who finance it.

B. Legislative Recommendations

Any amendment to the current law should control the supply of tickets in the secondary or resale market. An additional goal should be to increase the flow of information to the public through disclosure regarding the number of tickets actually available for general sale to the public and through measures which attempt to assure members of the public a fairer deal when they buy tickets.

More specifically, the following statutory changes should be enacted:

* Increasing criminal sanctions and the persons subject to them including:
  i. increasing paying or receiving ice to a felony level offense;
  ii. including promoters as persons prohibited from receiving ice;
  iii. prohibiting Treasurers and Assistant Treasurers from withholding tickets from sale to the general public without the express authorization of the owner or operator of the place of entertainment.

iv. creating a new subdivision under the section dealing with ticket speculation for persons who sell more than 20 tickets to an event or when the amount charged for tickets to one event totals more than $1000, making such activity a felony level offense.

* Granting the Attorney General the authority to obtain:
  i. injunctive relief;
  ii. court ordered disclosure in conjunction with a preliminary injunction;
  iii. civil penalties and an additional allowance.

* Centralizing registration and enforcement authority with respect to the sale, resale, allocation and distribution of tickets in the Attorney General's Office; and

* An increase of the maximum premium price inclusive of any service charges, delivery fees and membership fees. The maximum premium price should be high enough to bring licensed New York ticket brokers whose prices are not inflated by the payment of ice under the statutory scheme;

* A requirement that the initials or other identifying code of the individual ticket seller who sold the ticket and an individual serial number be printed on the face of each ticket.

* Prohibiting ticket resellers from hiring and using "diggers" to stand on line to buy tickets for resellers to sell.

* Requiring ticket sellers to register with the Department of Taxation and Finance and to pay taxes on the resale price of a ticket, including all fees and service charges.

* Requiring disclosure to a potential purchaser concerning the percentage of tickets available for public sale, including tickets to sporting events that have been purchased by season ticket holders, and information about access to season tickets; in the case of legitimate theatres, requiring disclosure of the number of house

seats, as well as disclosure of when the house seats are released for general sale.
* Making tickets sold as part of a travel package subject to ACAL.
* Establishing additional ticket disclosure requirements for sellers and resellers of tickets with respect to location of seat, any added fees or charges and refund policy.
* Establishing a refund policy for ticket resellers comparable to that for operators of places of entertainment.
* Elimination of the provisions requiring ticket resellers to obtain a certificate for each ticket location and requiring the posting of their license or certificate.

In sum, New York should pass a ticket resale law that increases the Attorney General's authority to investigate; that contains meaningful civil enforcement provisions; and contains sufficient penalties to deter criminal activities. Moreover, the law should be updated to reflect the current realities and the new technologies in the ticket resale business—a enormous changes with which the law has not kept abreast.

VII. CONCLUSION

For 77 years New York has legislatively regulated both the resale and the resellers of tickets. Yet, it has not succeeded in eliminating the abuse the law was intended to address. Although there has been repeated incremental change of the law, the goal of creating a fairer ticket distribution system that provides access to New York entertainment and sports events to average consumers at reasonable prices remains elusive. What has evolved is a complex network of persons actively deriving huge profits from the resale of tickets and a system of ticket distribution that favors wealthy individuals and firms with access to entertainment and sports events that is denied or greatly limited to ordinary fans and tourists.

This report is intended to shine light on an underground economy that persists because of a general lack of knowledge of the degree of the criminal activity involved. It is not just ticket scalping—it is bribery and tax evasion on a grand scale. In addition to violations of law, it involves inequity such as the massive diversion of tickets to insiders and people with connections, whether as a result of fraudulent activity or otherwise. This report is intended to enhance public awareness of the nature and extent of the problem and to promote effective legislation. New York, the entertainment capital of the world, should pass a ticket resale law that provides sufficient protection to the public.

Finally, there is more that owners and operators of theatres, concert and sports venues can do, either individually or through organization, to police their own industry. The industry is better placed than government agencies to root out corruption and to set up standards and guidelines for itself and its employees. Decreasing the number of house seats and strictly controlling their distribution is just one example of an action that venues can undertake. Industry action to deter fraudulent and unfair ticket distribution practices will ultimately benefit the public, as well as the industry.

---

1. N.Y. Arts & Cult. Aff. Law § 25.11 (McKinney 1984 & Supp. 1997).

2. "Scalping is no longer merely the province of individuals who . . . sell [tickets] for a huge profit on the sidewalk" but also of "[t]icket wholesalers [who] buy up huge blocks of

tickets and resell them at illegally high prices." Editorial, Broadway Robbery, N.Y. Times, Mar. 25, 1995, § 1, at 22.

3. N.Y. Arts & Cult. Aff. Law § 25.13 prohibits reselling or engaging in the business of reselling tickets without first procuring a license from the commissioner of licenses of the political subdivision in which such business will be conducted. In New York City, the Commissioner of Consumer Affairs performs the function of issuing licenses to ticket resellers. Many New York localities, however, do not have anyone who performs this function. One suggestion has been that all licensing of ticket brokers should be with the Secretary of State, rather than local municipalities. See May 1995 Comm. Hearing (testimony of New York City Commissioner of Consumer Affairs, Alfred C. Cerullo, III). Commissioner Cerullo noted that "ticket brokers typically do not limit sales to residents of a single municipality" and that they "can easily relocate when targeted for prosecution at the local level." Since ticket brokers conduct their business across county lines, as well as state lines, uniform, centralized licensing and supervision by the State of New York would be appropriate. As an alternative to central licensing with the Secretary of State, legislative consideration should be given to placing this authority with the Attorney General, along with increased enforcement powers. See Legislative Recommendations Section, infra.

4. For example, those who advertise in the New York media have New York telephone numbers, sell tickets to New York events to New York consumers for delivery in New York.

5. By defining "resale" as including sales "where either buyer or seller is located in this state," the 1991 amendment of Article 25 clearly affirmed New York's jurisdiction over resellers who

do business in New York or who sell tickets to New York customers, but attempt to evade the law by locating their offices outside New York's borders. See N.Y. Arts & Cult. Aff. Law § 25.03(9).

6. In the heart of the theatre district at Eighth Avenue and 46th Street is a tavern by the name of McHale's which is a well-known "drop" for tickets. Tickets are left there in envelopes, for brokers who send messengers to pick them up. There is constant traffic of this nature, as observed by undercover investigators of the Attorney General.

7. Manhattan Theatre Ticket Service, Inc. is a New York entity which is affiliated with Manhattan Entertainment, Inc., a New Jersey entity. According to accounting records obtained by the Attorney General's Office pursuant to the execution of a search warrant in September, 1994, the New Jersey entity made deposits to the New York entity for the exact dollar amount that the New York entity was paying for tickets over a substantial period of time. See also, letter to Manhattan Ticket Service c/o Manhattan Entertainment, Inc. regarding bond renewals, Exhibit A. Such information demonstrates that Manhattan Theatre Ticket Service, Inc. and Manhattan Entertainment, Inc. were, in fact, operating as a single entity.

8. They charge over the maximum premium price, but they rely upon an opinion of the Law Department of the City of New York which interpreted the law as permitting ticket brokers reasonable charges for extra services actually performed.

9. The three dominant ones are: Applause Theatre & Entertainment Service, Inc., Theatre Service Americana, and Golden, Penn, Le Blanq Theatre Ticket Service.

10. See Public Hearing on Ticket Scalping: Before Assembly Comm. On Tourism, Arts & Sports Development 65, 322 (Aug. 16, 1994) [hereinafter Hearing (Aug. 16, 1994)](testimony of Allan Zelnick, Esq., on behalf of Theater Service Americana and Arthur Golden of Golden, Penn, Le Blanq Theatre Ticket Service.)

11. Statements of hotel concierges and others.

12. Hearing (Aug. 16, 1994), at 322-26.

13. Many premium brokers have stopped doing business with individual New York purchasers or will tell individual callers that they cannot deliver tickets in New York.

14. Jim Evans, "On the Net, Everyone Can Be a Scalper," The Industry Standard, May 3, 1999.

15. *Id.*

16. *Id.*

17. *Id.*

18. *A large number of box office employees are related to employees at other box offices, such as five brothers who worked at five different Broadway box offices (one is retired, but a son of one of them has come into the business). Many such ticket selling families also have relatives in ticket brokerage firms. Some box office employees and theatre insiders, however, by-pass this familial route entirely and just become ticket brokers themselves. For example, an employee of the Nederlander Organization who most recently worked in the box office of the Nederlander*

Theatre (where "Rent" is playing), worked at Global Travel and Entertainment in Comack, New York and as a ticket seller at Radio City Music Hall at the same time.

19. *As noted below, the subject matter jurisdiction of New York law is based on the location of either the buyer or the seller of tickets. New Jersey, by contrast, derives its jurisdiction over the resale of tickets on the basis of the location of the event, i.e., it has jurisdiction only over ticket resales to New Jersey events. That is why ticket resellers located in New Jersey selling tickets to New York events arguably are not subject to New Jersey law.*

20. *Noted Broadway producer David Merrick stated during his testimony [Inquiry by Hon. Louis J. Lefkowitz, Attorney General of N.Y., into Financing and Ticket Distribution Practices in N.Y. Legitimate Theatre, Dec. 10, 1963] that the derivation of the word ice in this connection was based on two possible sources: (1) that such payments were recorded on ice that "melted away," or (2) a turn of the century political expression for items listed as "incidental campaign expenses" (i.c.e.). Orestes J. Mihaly & David J. Kaufman, Practice Commentary, N.Y. Arts & Cult. Aff. Law tit F, Art. 23 n.2 (McKinney 1984 & Supp. 1997).*

21. *"Resale" is defined as "any sale of a ticket other than a sale by the operator or the operator's agent who is expressly authorized to make first sales of such tickets." N.Y. Arts & Cult. Aff Law § 25.03(9). Computerized ticket services such as Ticketmaster are considered agents of the operator or original sellers of tickets under this definition.*

22. *Exhibit F is a document obtained in September, 1994 by the Attorney General's office at the premises of an illegal New York ticket broker, Redmark Entertainment. New York theatres are*

listed in the column on the left; on the right is a column showing the amount of ice required to obtain tickets at certain theatres, ranging from $20 for "Three Tall Women" (which was playing at the off-Broadway, Promenade Theatre) to $35 for "Beauty and the Beast," "Angels in America," "Grease," and "Tommy" at the Palace Theatre, Walter Kerr Theatre , Eugene O'Neill Theatre, and St. James Theatre, respectively.

23. *ACAL § 25.03(4).*

24. *For further discussion of this issue, see Andrew Kandel & Elizabeth Block, The De-Icing of Ticket Prices: A Proposal Addressing the Problem of Commercial Bribery in the New York Ticket Industry, 5 J.L. & Pol'y 489 (1997).*

25. A-7480.

26. N.J. Stat.Ann. § 56:8-27 to 39 (West 1989)

27. Memorandum of Governor Christine Todd Whitman to the Senate (June 19, 1995).

28. Report to Governor Christine Todd Whitman on "Access To Entertainment In New Jersey", at 16-17.

29. Subsequent to the Attorney General's inquiry regarding the distribution of tickets to "The Lion King", the ticket sales policy was changed with respect to Ticketmaster telephone and outlet sales to permit the purchase of 19 tickets per performance to two separate performances. Alan Levey, Vice President and General Manager of Walt Disney Productions, gave testimony at the Attorney General's Office on March 26, 1998. The exchange between him and Assistant Attorney General Elizabeth Block is attached as Exhibit H.

30. Jacob's did not receive either show; Green's was not on the list for "Grease."

31. Applause, Golden LeBlanq, Liberty, Allied, Edwards and Edwards and Keith Prouse.

32. *See Exhibit J. Philip Molite testified at a hearing at the Attorney General's Office on March 18, 1998. See Exhibit K. At that time he had been the Ticket Manager at the USA National Tennis Center for twenty years. His employment was terminated several months after this hearing for reasons unrelated to his conduct as Ticket Manager. Mr. Molite acknowledged that he personally had sold a 1997 season subscription to Manhattan Entertainment, contrary to the stated policy of his employer. However he offered as explanation that absent a complaint that such seats were being offered by the broker at an "excessive amount" neither he nor the USA would have taken them off a list of long time subscribers. This is an astonishing response in view of the number of complaints and the level of outcry that reached the Attorney General's Office and the media in relation to the scarcity of seats (other than ground passes) and the unfairness of the distribution process in 1997.*

33. *Ice is generally acknowledged privately among persons in the sports and entertainment business. In public, references to it are more guarded. Gerald Schoenfeld, Chairman of the Shubert Organization testified on August 16, 1994 before the Assembly Committee on Tourism, Arts & Sports Development that among the methods used by scalpers to obtain tickets is the "attempt to bribe ticket vendor personnel to sell them tickets or give advance notice when new inventories of tickets are being released for sale." See Public Hearing on Ticket Scalping: Hearing Before*

Assembly Comm. On Tourism, Arts & Sports Development, 177 (Aug. 16, 1994) [hereinafter Hearing (Aug. 16, 1994)].

34. *One persistent rumor among industry insiders is that over the ten years of its run, the ice paid on "Phantom of the Opera" tickets exceeded its net profits—the basis for calculating the proceeds of most creative people and investors.*

35. *Joseph Nekola, the Jones Beach Marine Theatre ("Jones Beach") treasurer—who pled guilty to a felony involving his receipt of ice in People v. Nekola—and other former and current Jones Beach ticket sellers worked at Madison Square Garden ("MSG") during non-summer months; two ticket sellers whose employment at MSG was terminated pursuant to an internal investigation were thereafter employed by the Nederlander organization; two others terminated by Radio City Music Hall were thereafter employed by the Shubert Organization and the Nederlander Organization.*

36. *Ticketmaster does not provide the ticket seller at the venue box office, but it does provide the box office terminals.*

37. *According to Ticketmaster, approximately 60 percent of its sales in the Northeast region are transacted over the telephone.*

38. *The Rite Aid contract was recently terminated.*

39. *According to Ticketmaster, such independent stores currently account for only about five percent of its outlets.*

40. *Hearing (Aug. 16, 1994), Transcript at 21-26.*

41. *The same method can be used at a box office or telephone center.*

42. *"Diggers" may be used at theatres, as well as at concerts, for a particular hot show such as The Lion King. A New Jersey ticket "wholesaler" who is known to specialize in The Lion King tickets uses diggers to augment his own purchases and those of his employees. This broker was able to obtain approximately 700 tickets over a ten day period when the box office first opened for sale. Generally, theatre box offices sell tickets for up to a year in advance and extend that period in three month increments. Thus, as of this writing, The Lion King tickets are available through the spring of 2000. Undoubtedly, this period shortly will be extended through September or October of 2000. At the time such new tickets are put on sale, those persons in the know—primarily ticket brokers—will attempt through the use of diggers, as well as family and friends, to purchase the best Saturday night (and in the case of The Lion King, Saturday matinee) seats in the new batch of tickets.*

43. *The distinction between theatre party agents and group sales agents has grown somewhat fuzzy over the years. In fact, many such agents, including the biggest, wear both hats. Theoretically, theatre party agents are the selling agents for the theatre to charitable organizations, which may resell tickets without any price restriction, solely for fund-raising purposes. Charitable organizations are generally only interested in musical productions and only during the first three or four months when a show is considered hot. If the party is large enough, there is an automatic reduction of house seats to make them available to the theatre party. Theatre party agents have the right to return up to 25 percent of unsold tickets to the theatre. These returned tickets may be sold to brokers. Although technically prohibited by their contract with the theatre from selling to ticket brokers, theatre party agents may dispose of these highly desirable tickets.*

Group sales agents may sell to any group of 20 or more persons. No screening of the purchasers takes place, so ticket brokers occassionally purchase tickets in this way. If the group is large enough, there may also be an automatic reduction of house seats to make them available for the group. Although, as with theatre parties, the contract prohibits sale to brokers, there is no enforcement mechanism to prevent this.

44. One creative entrepreneur proposed to the United Way of New York City ("United Way") that he would run a ticket service for it (for which United Way would compensate him on a commission basis) to avoid the restrictions governing the resale of tickets in New York. Noting the amount of money to be made in the ticket resale business, he estimated that the United Way could net between $500,000 and $1,000,000 annually from this project. United Way declined to become involved.

45. This number varies depending on the size of the theatre and may be changed during the run of a show. For *The Lion King*, it was 250 when the show began; it currently is 300.

46. Actually, the number of hours prior to the performance at which house seats are released is scheduled on a "time-release" basis, so that portions are released 72 hours prior to the performance, 48 hours prior to the performance and 24 hours prior to the performance. A small number of such seats are held until just prior to the performance for last minute "V.I.P.s" and for other emergencies. For concerts, there is generally a specified time prior to the performance by which reserved tickets must be released for sale to the general public.

47. How the remainder of such tickets were distributed has not yet been ascertained, although it appears that being a Knicks or Rangers subscriber was helpful. Twenty-eight Spice Girls management holds were sold to Knicks or Rangers subscribers. Interestingly, 16 management holds went to treasurers and ticket sellers at other box offices, including four seats each to two employees at *The Lion King* box office—even though MSG's own box office employees were limited to two tickets each.

48. Interviews of persons sitting in seats allocated to Delsener/ Slater at the July 1, 1998 Spice Girls concert at MSG revealed that at least 24 of those seat holders had obtained their tickets from ticket brokers.

49. A list of contacts seized pursuant to the execution of a search warrant by the New York and New Jersey Attorneys General at the premises of Herman Agar, Co. contained the name of the coordinator of Delsener/Slater's Club.

50. An August 3, 1997 New York Post expose under the banner, "What an Outrage! Ticket seeking VIPs," provided what it called a "top-secret" list of select Knicks ticket-seekers from 1993 to 1996. Both lists, the article stated, are broken into five parts, Priority 1 through Priority 5. Only the Priority 1 list was published. It shows the name of the person seeking the ticket and the results—generally upgrade or granted, but in some cases the ticket seeker preferred waiting for better seats. A third column on the list is reserved for comments. It indicates which management person made the request and sometimes contains explanations for the request, e.g., the ticket-seeker is a relative of a well-known person or perhaps,

his dentist. The existence of such management lists and their contents is, in substance, confirmed by the Attorney General's investigation.

51. Some of the persons terminated by MSG were simply hired as box office employees in other organizations such as Broadway theatres.

52. In this instance, the Attorney General was not aware of the misconduct until the termination was reported in the normal course of business on a ticket distributor registration form. The Arts and Cultural Affairs Law provides for an administrative procedure to revoke the ticket distributor registration of an employee in control of the distribution or allocation of tickets for box office conduct that operates as a fraud upon the public. The same law also makes it a crime to exact, demand, accept or receive any premium in excess of the regular or established price of the ticket. N.Y. Arts & Cult. Aff. Law §§23.23 and 25.29. If evidence of such misconduct is not brought to the Attorney's General's attention, however, even employees terminated for cause can simply move to another venue.

53. *See Public Hearing on Ticket Scalping: Hearing Before Assembly Comm. On Tourism, Arts & Sports Development 64, 322 (Aug. 16, 1994) (testimony of Gerald Schoenfeld).*

54. *See Public Hearing on Ticket Scalping: Hearing Before Assembly Comm. on Tourism, Arts & Sports Development 64, 322 (Aug. 16, 1994) (testimony of John DeRosa).*

55. *People v. Rosenblatt, N.Y.L.J., (col.3) Jan. 25, 1999 at 29.*

56. *Id.*

57. *Id.*

58. *Id.*

Bibliography

Who Goes to Broadway? The Demographics of the Audience 2002-2003. By Karen Hauser. Published by The League of American Theatres and Producers, Inc., New York, NY. Copyright © October 2003. ISBN 0-972-0527-3-9.

The Audience for Touring Broadway – A Demographic Study 2001-2002. By Karen Houser. Published by The League of American Theatres and Producers, Inc., New York, NY. Copyright © April 2003. ISBN 0-972-0527-2-0.

The New York Times Company Inc. Various articles and reviews 2000-2004 by columnists Frank Rich, Ben Brantley, Jason Zinoman, Bruce Webber, Jesse McKinley, Zachary Pincus-Roth, Lawrence Van Gelder, Julie Salamon, Benedict Nightingale. Copyright © 2000-2004. All Rights Reserved.

Playbill On-Line's Brief Encounter with Harold Prince. Robert Simonson – October 22, 2002. Copyright © 2003. All Rights Reserved.

Playbill On-Line's Brief Encounter with Cameron Mackintosh. Kenneth Jones – December 10, 2003. Coyright © 2003. All Rights Reserved.

Playbill OnLine—Various articles 2000-2004 by columnists Andrew Gans, James Inverne, Ernio Hernandez.

B*roadway.com* – A division of Hollywood Media Corp. Various articles, columns, and commentaries by Ken Mandelbaum, Cara Joy David.

OffBroadwayOnLine.com—The official website of Off-Broadway. Copyright © 2003 The Alliance of Resident Theatres New York. All Rights Reserved.

Why Can't I Get Tickets? A report from the Office of new York State Attorney General Eliot Spitzer. The Bureau of Investor Protection and Securities. Copyright © 1999.

Variety and Variety.com—Various articles 2000-2004 by columnists Robert Hofler, Charles Isherwood, Matt Wolf, Charles Newberry. Copyright © 2000-2004. All Rights Reserved.

The Sunday Times of London—Various articles 2000-2004 by columnist John Peters. Copyright © 2000-2004. All Rights Reserved.

The Evening Standard—Various articles 2000-2004 by columnist Nick Curtis. Copyright © 2000-2004. All Rights Reserved.

Special Thanks and

Acknowledgments . . .

There are many people responsible for the writing of this book. Most of them—professionally, as well as because of their endearing friendship over the years—have greatly contributed to my professional success. I would like to thank them all, as well as the numerous authors I have admired over the years who—through their own writing skills—have encouraged me to take my experience and knowledge of producing theatre, and actually put pen to paper.

I would like to thank authors Frank Browning, Scott Heim, P.D. James, Diana Preston, and Russell Reich for encouraging me greatly throughout this process.

I would also like to thank producer Trent Rhoton—my colleague and longtime friend—whose early readings of this manuscript—and whose cogent comments and many suggestions—have improved this book immensely.

Special thanks must also go to the Xlibris Corporation—especially to Dave Weinman, Matt Griffin, Thomas McAteer, Beth Staples, and Jenn Faulk for their hard work, constant support, and overall encouragement.

And also to Cameron Mackintosh, Alan Wasser, Bob Mac Donald, Mary Thomas, Maritza Perez, Brett Bullock, David Stewardson, Michael Day, Rupert Sykes, Maurizio Eliseo, Anthony Cooke, Bill Miller, Bob Jani, Patricia Morinelli, Ken Billington, Howard Kolins, Greg DeFelice, Judy Carmichael, Jim Brochu, Steve Schalchlin, Jim Eisner, Brian Monahan, and Waldemar Hansen.

And finally—to Lyle Jones, Laurette De Rosairo, and Brian Beaton . . . for getting it all started in the first place.

Steven Rivellino
March 2004

About The Author

Steven Rivellino is an accomplished writer, lecturer, and producer of theatrical entertainment. He has worked successfully on both sides of the Atlantic—with credits spanning Broadway, Off-Broadway, television, and the corporate arena. From 1982 to 1990 he was Vice President and General Manager of Radio City Music Hall in New York—a time during which he produced *The Grammy Awards*, *The MTV Video Music Awards*, numerous concerts and special events, and of course the celebrated *Radio City Christmas Spectacular*.

A member of the Circumnavigators Club, he has traveled the world extensively—far north of the Arctic Circle, south to Antarctica; from the Greenwich Meridian, east to the International Date Line.

He lives in New York City and Cedar Lake New Jersey; and is currently at work on a full-length history of America's first and only nuclear-powered passenger vessel NS *Savannah*.

His first book—*Mysterious Places, Mysterious Dreams* (Xlibris)—successfully debuted in early 2004.

Notes on

Bright Lights, Big Changes

Art Direction and Cover Design for *Bright Lights, Big Changes* by Steven Rivellino and Trevor Crafts.

The interior text was set in 12-point Adobe Garamond—a typeface based on the sixteenth-century type designs of Claude Garamond, re-drawn by Robert Slimbach in 1989.

The original cover photograph entitled *Spotlight Shining On Empty Stage* is by G.K. & Vikki Hart.

§

www.brightlightsbigchanges.com